Sayuri's
Food for Yogi's &
Everyone

Sayuri's Vegan Cookbook series Vol. 1

Sayuri's Food for Yogi's & Everyone

Sayuri's Vegan Cookbook series Vol. 1

Sayuri Tanaka

Published by PT. Benih Hayati

First published 2015

ISBN: 978-602-71673-5-3 (Paperback)
ISBN: 978-602-71673-4-6 (ebook)

Published by PT. Benih Hayati
http://www.yummtumm.com • tanaka.sayuri@gmail.com
http://www.theseedsoflife.net (the Seeds of Life)
No2 Jalan Goutama, Ubud, Bali 80571 Indonesia

Photography : Sayuri Tanaka, (Kino & Tim's photo by Tom Rosenthal), Milla
Design: Sayuri Tanaka
Production: Darlene Swanson
Proofreading : Jody Amato

This book is dedicated to my beautiful friends,
whom I have come across in my journey around the world.

I further dedicate this to my dearest mother and father,
who have given me infinite love, which has always
been the source of my love within and in my food.

This is also dedicated to you, whom I luckily
came across through this book.

Love and gratitude,

Sayuri

2015

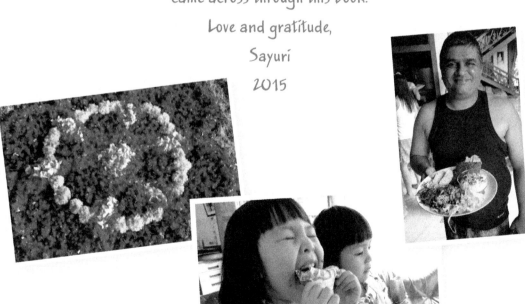

Contents

About the Author

Sayuri Tanaka
Retreat Chef & Raw Food Trainer

As a raw/vegan/macrobiotic chef and teacher, Sayuri offers individuals an experience of what it's truly like for the body to be nourished and the heart to be opened through her food. As a teacher, she demonstrates the simplicity of physical and spiritual transformation through food. This knowledge has taken her around the world to share with others for decades. A yoga practitioner herself, Sayuri has catered for yoga retreats in India, Bali, Australia, North and South America, and Europe, and studied at some of the great academies and institutes of raw food and macrobiotics, which has given her a greater understanding of preparing foods for yogis' individual needs.

Sayuri encourages and promotes a healthy, sustainable, and highly conscious lifestyle for all of us, the earth, and the future through teaching the healthy way of eating and training around the world, and by sharing the love and knowledge she has within.

As yoga transforms you, so does her food—guaranteed!

Sayuri Tanaka

www.yummtumm.com (English)
www.sayuritanaka.com (Japanese)
www.theseedsoflife.net
tanaka.sayuri@gmail.com

Foreword

I have finally put together a collection of the most popular, easiest, and yet yummiest and healthiest recipes that have been enjoyed by many yogis and yoginis whom I have been cooking for in retreat centres around the world. I have kept all the recipes vegan and noted alternatives for people who have allergies to certain foods, so everyone can enjoy the entire menu!

Using lots of fresh fruits and vegetables, beans, tofu, tempeh, nuts, and seeds, I have strived to satisfy not just vegans, but also non-vegans and vegetarians. Raw, living foods are also introduced here and there in the recipes. For men who need satisfying meals, for kids and elders who need fun and gentle meals, and of course for busy women who need simple and easy preparation, this recipe book is suitable for everyone!

My philosophy of cooking is to be creative, especially with vegan and raw food. You may think, "Oh, I don't have this and that so I cannot make this and that" . . . Nooooope! If your imagination is unlimited, your cooking can be as well. In fact, the dishes you create include so much of you. Remember, the recipes are just guidelines. Don't worry too much about them and be experimental with measures and flavours to achieve the taste that is right for you. Each person has different tastes and needs, so play with ingredients or what is available to you.

It is very important to choose organic ingredients whenever possible. By doing so, you are making a stand against damaging our bodies and the Earth with toxins and chemicals, as well as supporting organic farmers. By choosing a vegan diet, you are also helping to protect animals from cruelty and saving the limited resources of our planet.

Preparing the food in a harmonious way will not only make you feel good, it will also help those who eat your creations to connect with nature. Isn't it wonderful to be a bridge between those two?

I am blessed to have been given this opportunity to cook for people in this way. It is an absolute joy and privilege for me. It's been nourishment for me to see the smiles on my friends' faces whenever they enjoy my culinary creations!

This book was created to share the joy of cooking, especially cooking for others. I hope your body, mind, and spirit will be nourished through the food made with love.

So have fun and enjoy cooking! Make yourself happy, make people around you happy and full, and make the world better! Make our future beautiful! Yes, your choice of food does matter! As yoga transforms you, I guarantee you that good food equally transforms you and the world!

The Many Varieties of Vegetarians

Although the word "vegetarian" is widely understood to describe those who do not eat animal products, originally it comes from the Latin word "vegetus," meaning lively and vigorous, with the suffix "-arian." [1]

Many choose this diet for health, ethical, religious, and many other reasons, and often it encompasses their way of living, with individual beliefs and ethics of nonviolence, animal rights, environmental issues, etc.

Vegans, strict vegetarians, do not eat food derived from animals even indirectly, such as dairy products, eggs, and honey. Many vegans have a rigid philosophy on animal rights, and even avoid wearing leather, wool, silk, and down that is made from animals, and cosmetics that are tested on animals.[2] Many vegans believe strongly in an environmentally sustainability world, as industrial farming of animals is environmentally damaging and unsustainable.

Macrobiotics is the practicatl application of the natural laws of change; the constantly changing nature of all things. A basic tenet of macrobiotic thinking is that all things are composed of yin energy (outward moving) and yang energy (inward). The macrobiotic approach to diet emphasizes whole grains and fresh vegetables, which make it easier to achieve a more balanced condition within the natural order of life.[3]

There are also other vegetarian diets: a pescetarian diet includes fish; a lacto-vegetarian diet includes dairy products, an ovo-vegetarian diet includes eggs, etc. In Hinduism, the Indian pure vegetarian diet includes dairy products, but not eggs; in Buddhism, Japanese traditional vegetarian monk food is basically vegan.

A raw, living-food diet includes high percentages of live, unheated, unprocessed foods, such as whole fruits, vegetables, seaweeds, nuts and seeds, fermented foods and sprouted foods. Although some raw food enthusiasts eat animal products, the raw food that I share in this book is vegan. By eating highly vibrational, nutritionally dense food, we achieve harmony with nature and health in body, mind, and spirit. As well as vegetarian, vegan, and macrobiotic, this is not just a diet, but reflects a way of life, thought, philosophy, and ethics.

Although there are many types of vegetarians, please find the way of eating that you need according to your age, life stage, feelings, and emotions in the moment, seasons, climate, and way of life. Gradually, you will become aware that food affects your thoughts and behaviors, as well as everything happening around you. If the food makes your body, mind, and spirit happy, inevitably the Earth and all living beings become happy and healthy. Our bodies are a reflection of the universe, so taking good care of the inner microcosms of ourselves leads to the health of the outer macrocosms.

In any diet, "good food" is, in my opinion, the food that is harmonious with nature and allows us to be aligned with the universal energy, and encourages the body's natural ability to heal and rebuild itself.

References:

1. " Vegetarianism." Wikipedia: The Free Encyclopedia, Nov 11 2014, 19:33 UTC.
   < http://en.wikipedia.org/wiki/Vegetarianism >

2. " Veganism." Wikipedia: The Free Encyclopedia, Nov 15 2014, 09:26 UTC.
   < http://en.wikipedia.org/wiki/Veganism >

3. Ferre, Carl. "What is Macrobiotics?" George Ohsawa Macrobiotic Foundation, 2011. 15 Sep 2014
   < http://www.ohsawamacrobiotics.com/macrobiotics/what-is-macrobiotics >

Important Notes Before Starting

Basic Measurement Standard

1 cup = 250ml

1/2 cup = 125ml

1/4 cup = 60ml = 4 tablespoons

1 tablespoon = 15ml

1 teaspoon = 5ml

1 oz. by weight = 30 grams

1 inch = 2.54 cm

> **FYI:** Measurement of nuts and seeds are before soaking. When you measure after soaking, measure 1.2-2 times more, as it increases the volume.

FYI: Ounces (oz.) are measured by weight, not by volume. When measured by volume, it is noted as such. Each recipe is for 4-6 servings, unless otherwise mentioned.

Ingredient Alternatives

My ingredient choices are a collection from all the recipes I have created throughout my travels in many different parts of the world. If some ingredients are unavailable or hard to find, try replacing them with ingredients you're familiar with to create your own original recipe! Here are some examples of alternatives.

Ingredients	Alternatives
Macadamia nuts	Cashew nuts
White miso	Nutritional yeast
Galangal	Ginger
Zucchini	Turnip
Pecan nuts	Walnuts
Flaxseed oil	Olive oil
Coconut oil	Grape seed oil or sunflower oil

For more on finding ingredients, see the **Kitchen Staples and Vegan Alternatives** on page 16.

Basic Ingredient Term Conversion

Some ingredients are called by different names from country to country. Here are the common ingredient names, which are often confused. In this book, I am using the ones that I am familiar with.

In This Book	Other Terms
Cilantro	Fresh Coriander Leaf
Eggplant	Aubergine
Chickpea	Garbanzo Bean
Green Onion	Scallion, Spring Onion
Snow Pea	Mangetout
Zucchini	Courgette
Arugula	Rocket, rucola
Bell Pepper	(Sweet) paprika, (Sweet) Pepper, Capsicum
Bean Shoot	Bean Sprout

How to Substitute for Wheat Flour

This is the general way to substitute wheat flour with wheat-free or/and gluten-free flour.

Just replace 1 cup of wheat flour with 1 cup of wheat-free flour.

When replacing with wheat-free and gluten-free flours, you need to add some "binder" (for vegan cooking—not when you are using eggs, which will be the binder). To replace 1 cup of wheat flour with wheat-free and gluten-free flours, use 7/8-3/4 cup of one of the those flours + 2-4 tablespoons one of the following binders.

Wheat-Free but contains some gluten	Spelt flour, oat flour, barley flour, rye flour
Wheat-Free & Gluten-Free	Amaranth flour, buckwheat flour, chickpea (garbanzo bean) flour, cornmeal, millet flour, potato flour, quinoa flour, rice flour, brown rice flour, soy flour
Binder	Potato starch, corn flour, kudzu (arrowroot powder), tapioca flour (cassava root powder)

FYI: When replacing wheat flour with wheat-free and gluten-free flours, you may need a bit more baking powder. Rice flour and cornmeal may have a bit of grainy texture. Since those alternative flours do not rise like wheat flour; when making muffins it may be better to make them in small sizes.

EQUIPMENT AND FUN GADGETS

Basic tools

Good knives and cutting boards

Spatulas

Mixing bowls and strainers

Measuring cups and measuring spoons

Scale

Whisk

Peeler

Slicer

Bamboo mat to roll sushi

Pots, pans, and saucepans

Oven, parchment paper (baking paper), pie pan*, tart pan*, cake tin*, muffin mould

Nut milk bag or cheesecloth to make nut milk

Simple recipe book you love

 * A 9-inch/23cm pie pan, tart pan, and cake tin are used in this book.

Equipment

High power blender (such as Vitamix or Blentech): I make most of the recipes with it! It is your first and most expensive gadget, but totally worth it to a have fun and a healthy, vibrant life!

Food processer (such as Cuisinart, KitchenAid or Robot Coupe): to make pate, paste, cakes, and cookies. You can start with any (cheap!) food processor before you invest in a more costly one.

Nice to have

Juicer (such as Champion, Green Star): it is not used in this book, but a great gadget for your optimum health! I recommend a cold press juicer for better taste and more nutrition.

Spiral slier (Spiralizer): to have fun spiralizing any vegetables into noodles.

Salad spinner: to make your salad nice and tasty. Makes a big difference!

Where to find equipment

www.vitamix.com (Vitamix blender)

www.blendtec.com (Blendtec blender)

www.cuisinart.com (Cuisinart food processor)

www.kitchenaid.com (KitchenAid food processor)

www.amazon.com or any amazon website for your country

www.discountjuicers.com

www.rawguru.com

Kitchen Staples and Vegan Alternatives

Selecting good-quality ingredients is a must. For produce, choose fresh, organic, local, and seasonal whenever possible. They have not only more nutritional value and taste, but are more healthy and friendly to the ecosystem. It is a choice between supporting local organic farmers or the mass food industry, and also whether you want to invest in your health and longevity that bring you happiness and success on many levels, or if you want to pay more later for the treatment and insurance for all variety of un-wellness.

Our choices are greatly responsible for our future.

Saltiness: Himalayan rock salt, Celtic sea salt, soy sauce (including nama-shoyu or tamari), white miso, and dark miso

Choose unrefined natural salt such as Himalayan rock salt or Celtic sea salt.

Use tamari for a gluten-free option.

White miso is great to recreate cheesy-ness, while dark miso helps to recreate meaty-ness.

Oil and butter: olive oil, sesame oil, coconut oil, flax seed oil, grape seed oil, sunflower oil, almond butter, peanut butter, and tahini

Choose unrefined, cold-pressed oil.

For desserts, I like to use coconut oil, unroasted sesame oil, or grape seed oil.

FYI: For cooking, I recommend using the oil that has a high smoke point (but not commercial high-heat extracted oil! Choose cold pressed. Use coconut oil, avocado oil, and olive oil for lower-heat cooking, if at all), because heating oil above the point produces toxins and becomes harmful. It is best not to heat oils too high.

For non-cooking, like salad dressings and garnishing, you may want to include oils that have healthy balanced Omega 3 and 6 fatty acids (e.g., flax seed oil, chia seed oil, and hemp seed oil), which are more heat sensitive and are known for their anti-inflammatory properties and promote cardiovascular heath.

Although I use certain oils in these recipes, please choose the one that you need, considering where you are, your preference, and cooking purpose.

Sourness: Apple cider vinegar, rice vinegar, wine vinegar, balsamic vinegar, and lemon juice

Sweetness: Maple syrup, dates, coconut sugar, molasses, unrefined cane sugar, and stevia.

Choose less-refined sweeteners whenever possible.

> **FYI:** Refined white sugar, the most common sugar on the table, makes your body extremely acidic and out of balance physically and mentally, requiring the minerals in the body to fix the imbalance. whole or less-refined natural sweeteners are great alternatives to refined white sugar, and have some nutritional values.

Although I use certain sweeteners in these recipes, please feel free to use any natural sweetener available, according to your need and location.

Grains and Flours: Brown rice, quinoa, millet, amaranth, couscous, pasta, soba noodles, rice noodles, oats, wheat flour, spelt flour, buckwheat flour, rice flour, rice paper, and spring roll sheet

Choose whole or less-refined grains and freshly stoned ground grains whenever possible.

FYI: for the wheat flour alternatives, see **How to Substitute for Wheat Flour** on page 13.

Beans and Legumes: Chickpea, kidney beans, broad beans, adzuki beans, black beans, lentil, mung beans, dhal, glass noodles, tofu, and tempeh

Milk: Nut or seed milk, soy milk, rice milk, and coconut milk

Dry goods: Nori, hijiki, wakame, arame, kombu, and shiitake mushrooms

Nuts and seeds: Almonds, cashew nuts, coconuts, macadamia nuts, pine nuts, pumpkin seeds, sunflower seeds, walnuts, and sesame seeds

Choose raw whenever possible; if unavailable, choose non-fried, non-flavoured nuts and seeds.

Almonds are a staple to make almond milk.

Cashew nuts are a wonderful substitute for dairy; they make beautiful nut cheeses and creams.

Dried fruits: Dates, figs, raisins, and goji berries

Choose sulphur-free dried fruits.

Spices: Stock your favourite spices as staples. Here are my staples: cumin, coriander, chilli powder and flakes, herbs (such as basil, oregano, thyme, and rosemary) onion powder, paprika powder, curry powder, cinnamon, nutmeg, clove, and cardamom. Smoked paprika, smoked salt, and onion powder can be useful to make the dish unique in flavour, so they are always in my kitchen (and in my suitcase when I travel for cooking!).

Misc.: Kudzu (arrowroot powder) or agar (as a thickener instead of animal-derived gelatine), aluminium-free baking powder, nutritional yeast (for a cheesy flavour), cacao powder, sun-dried tomato, olives, and vanilla beans and flavour extracts

Where to Find Ingredients

Produce, such as fresh fruit and vegetables, is best purchased from the local organic market, health food store, or delivery service.

Seaweed, dry mushrooms, green tea powder, young coconut meat, and any Asian items can be found in an Asian or Chinese grocery store.

Nutritional Yeast

Aluminium-free Baking Powder

Agar Powder

Kuzu Root Starch

Purchase the staples from a local health food store or online store.

www.iherb.com or the iherb website for your country
www.amazon.com or the amazon website for to your country
navitasnaturals.com (raw nuts and seeds, superfoods)
www.rawguru.com (raw nuts and seeds, superfoods)
www.frontiercoop.com (bulk herbs, spices, teas)

Techniques and Preparation in Advance

Basic Almond Milk

In this book, I describe "soy/rice/nut milk" as an alternative to cow's milk. You can use any milk of your choice but, indeed, nut milk is the easiest and healthiest to make at home. It's so much tastier, fresher, and cheaper than what you can buy. So why don't we make it at home!

Ingredients

1   cup almonds, soaked in water for 8-12 hours, rinsed and drained

4   cups water

FYI: The basic ratio is 1:4 for nuts to water; use less or more water depending on the desired consistency. Enjoy the milk using any nuts and seeds you like and find your favourite!

1. Blend all in a blender until almonds are completely broken down and smooth.
2. Strain through a nut milk bag or cheesecloth.
3. Add a pinch of salt, a little sweetener of your choice, and vanilla extract if desired (optional).
4. It can be kept in the fridge for several days.

FYI: The pulp that remains after squeezing the milk can made into burgers or patties. If you don't know what to do with it right now, store it in the freezer and think about it later. It can be kept in the freezer for 1 month or more. It can be dried over a low temperature in the oven (or in a dehydrator) and then ground into powder that can be used as a flour alternative.

Firming Tofu

Many of the recipes call for firm tofu. When you buy, look for "Momen" -tofu or firm tofu, not "Kinu" -tofu or silken tofu. If it is soft, drain the excess liquid to create a firmer, denser texture.

To firm up your tofu, wrap the tofu in a paper towel or cheesecloth, then sandwich between two chopping boards. Place a weight on the top of the chopping board to drain well. The weight should not be too light or too heavy, as it will squash the tofu into soup. It will take 30 minutes-1 hour until it becomes about 1/3-1/2-inch in thickness.

Chopping or Mincing Vegetables

You can quicken the process by chopping vegetables in a food processor! Be careful not to overstuff the food processor. If it's too full, some vegetables won't get chopped. Also, avoid overprocessing, as you will get veggie puree instead of diced or chopped veggies.

Cut the vegetables into chunks and toss them into the food processor. Pulse several times until the veggies are chopped. Scrape down the vegetables rising up around the edges in between pulsing to ensure they are evenly chopped.

Minced Garlic in Oil

This is a great way to store peeled and chopped garlic!

Mince the garlic with a knife or food processor. I often use a food processor, as it takes just a few seconds. Transfer the garlic into a glass jar and add olive oil or the oil of your choice. Make sure it is covered with oil completely so that it will not discolor or go off. Store in the fridge. It can be kept in to fridge for 1 month or more.

FYI: This can be used for any recipes that require garlic. As a guideline, 1 clove of garlic can be replaced by ½-1 teaspoon of minced garlic in oil but, of course, it depends on your preference.

Liquid Sweetener (Sugar Syrup)

Making powder or granule sugar, such as coconut sugar, into liquid form is useful for substituting any liquid sugar, such as maple syrup. Also, it is easy to dissolve into other ingredients.

Blend 1 cup of powder or granule sugar with 1/3 cup water until completely dissolved in the blender. Alternatively, you can warm them up together in a pot until the sugar dissolves. It can be kept in the fridge for 1 month or more.

How to Cook Grains

Although you can do this easily in an electric cooker nowadays, there is something more beneficial from cooking them on the stove, something that gives them more of the nourishment to feed our hearts.

Rinse well and drain grains. (Soak overnight for hard grains. You can also toast grains before cooking for the nutty, flavourful, fluffy outcome.)

In a saucepan, add grains and water required (see **Grains Cooking Chart** on page 25), with a pinch of salt and bring to a boil.

Turn the heat down to a simmer and cook, covered, for the required time (see **Grains Cooking Chart** on page 25), or until all the water is absorbed.

FYI: Quinoa need to be rinsed well for 2-3 minutes to remove saponins, a natural and protective coating that gives a bitter flavour if not rinsed off.

FYI: Buckwheat is quick to absorb liquid, so only bring the water to a boil, then add the buckwheat. When the water returns to a boil, turn the heat down to simmer, cover with a lid, and cook for the required time.

Check the grains for tenderness. If they need more time, simmer for another 5-10 minutes. If all the water is absorbed at this stage, add ¼ cup water to simmer.

When the grains are tender, remove from the heat and let them rest for 10 minutes with the lid on.

Grains Cooking Chart

Note that this is just a guideline. The duration and quantity of water will vary depending on your stove.

GRAIN (1 cup dry)	WATER (cups)	COOK TIME	YIELD (cups)
Amaranth	2½	20-25 min.	2½
Barley, pearled	3	50-60 min.	3½
Barley, hulled	3	1 hr. 15 min.	3½
Barley, flakes	2	30-40 min.	2½
Buckwheat groats	2	15 min.	2½
Cornmeal (fine grind)	4-4½	8-10 min.	2½
Cornmeal (polenta, coarse)	4-4½	20-25 min.	2½
Millet, hulled	3-4	20-25 min.	3½
Oat groats	3	30-40 min.	3½
Oat, bran	2½	5 min.	2
Quinoa	2	15-20 min.	2 ¾
Rice, white sushi rice	1.15	15-20 min.	1½
Rice, brown basmati	2½	35-40 min.	3
Rice, brown, long grain	2½	45-55 min.	3
Rice, brown, short grain	2-2½	45-55 min.	3
Rice, wild	3	50-60 min.	4
Rye, berries	3-4	1 hr.	3
Rye, flakes	2	10-15 min.	3
Spelt	3-4	40-50 min.	2½
Wheat, whole berries	3	2 hrs.	2½
Wheat, couscous	1	5 min.	2
Wheat, cracked	2	20-25 min.	2¼
Wheat, bulgur	2	15 min.	2½

Source: www.vegparadise.com

How to Cook Beans and Legumes

Rinse well and drain beans and legumes.

Soak them in plenty of water for 8 hours or overnight in order to increase digestibility. (If you don't have the time to soak them, bring the beans to a boil for 3 minutes, remove from heat and let sit for 1 hour covered. Drain the liquid and continue as follows.) Small legumes such as mung beans, lentils, adzuki, and split peas don't require soaking.

Drain the water.

In a large pot, place soaked beans or legumes with plenty of fresh water and a piece of Kombu, which helps lessen gas production.

Bring to a boil and skim off the foam.

Turn the heat down to simmer, cover with a lid, and cook until tender. Cooking time depends on the size of the beans. In general, it takes 45-70 minutes after boiling. (See the **Beans and Legumes Cooking Chart** on page 27.) In order to boil evenly and quickly, add 1 cup of cold water once or twice while cooking.

Check them for tenderness by gently press one bean with your fingertips. It is ready if it is squashed easily. If they need more time, continue to simmer. If all the water is completely absorbed at this stage, add 1/4 cup water while they simmer.

FYI: 1 cup of dry beans will yield about 2-3 cups of cooked beans. When a recipe calls for cooked beans, cook half that amount of dried beans, or make lots and keep for another meal. Cooked beans and legumes can be kept for 1 week in the fridge or 1 month in the freezer.

When they are tender, remove from the heat and let rest for 10 minutes, covered with a lid.

Beans and Legumes Cooking Chart

Note that this is just a guideline. The duration and quantity of water will vary depending on your stove.

BEAN (1 cup dry)	WATER (cups)	COOK TIME	YIELD (cups)
Adzuki (Aduki)	4	45-55 min.	3
Black beans	4	1-1½ hrs.	2¼
Black-eyed peas	3	1 hr.	2
Cannellini (white kidney beans)	3	45 min.	2½
Cranberry beans	3	40-45 min.	3
Fava beans, skins removed	3	40-50 min.	1 ²/₃
Garbanzos (chickpeas)	4	1-3 hrs.	2
Great northern beans	3½	1½ hrs.	2 ²/₃
Green split peas	4	45 min.	2
Yellow split peas	4	1-1½ hrs.	2
Green peas, whole	6	1-2 hrs.	2
Kidney beans	3	1 hr.	2¼
Lentils, brown	2 1/4	45 min.-1 hr.	2¼
Lentils, green	2	30-45 min.	2
Lentils, red	3	20-30 min.	2-2½
Lima beans, large	4	45-1 hr.	2
Lima beans, small	4	50-60 min.	3
Lima beans, Christmas	4	1 hr.	2
Mung beans	2½	1 hr.	2
Navy beans	3	45-60 min.	2 ²/₃
Pink beans	3	50-60 min.	2 ³/₄
Pinto beans	3	1½ hrs.	2 ²/₃
Soybeans	4	3-4 hrs.	3

Source: www.vegparadise.com

DRINKS

Energize with fresh smoothies and cozy up with warm drinks!

Green Smoothie

Boosts you up for the day with green power!

Yield: serves 2-3

1½ cups water
2   cups frozen bananas
2   cups frozen pineapples
1-2 tablespoons green powder (spirulina, green barley, wheatgrass)

1. Blend all ingredients in a blender until smooth.

Mango Shake

Almost like a dessert. Delicious!

Yield: serves 2-3

2   cups soy/rice/nut milk
2½ cups frozen chopped mango
¼   teaspoon cardamom powder

1. Blend all ingredients in a blender until smooth.

Cacao Shake

A magical drink that makes everybody happy!

Yield: serves 2-3

2   cups soy/rice/nut milk
2½ cups frozen bananas
3   tablespoons cacao powder
1-2 tablespoons maple syrup
1   teaspoon vanilla extract

1. Blend all ingredients in a blender until smooth.

Strawberry and Goji Milkshake

This brings me back to my childhood—those sweet days!

Yield: serves 2-3

2   cups soy/rice/nut milk
1½ cups frozen strawberries
1   cup frozen bananas
2   tablespoons goji berries
1-2 tablespoons maple syrup

1. Blend all ingredients in a blender until smooth.

Spiced Hot Chocolate

Cacao's rich aroma and taste go well with spicy, stimulation cayenne pepper. A classic in Mexico.

Yield: serves 4

5   cups soy/rice/nut milk

5   tablespoons coconut sugar or sweetener of your choice

1   teaspoon cinnamon powder

pinch of cayenne pepper or chilli powder

5   tablespoons cacao powder

1   teaspoon vanilla extract

1. Blend all ingredients in a blender and pour into a saucepan, or whisk all together in a saucepan.
2. Turn the heat on and warm it up.

Milky Green Barley Tea

Green barley, my favourite superfood, tastes like green tea, yet mild and sweet. Delicious!

Yield: serves 4

5   cups soy/rice/nut milk
    sweetener of your choice

2   tablespoons green barley grass powder

3   tablespoons coconut sugar or

1. Blend all ingredients in a blender and pour into a saucepan, or whisk all together in a saucepan.
2. Turn the heat on and warm it up.

Masala Chai (Milk Tea with Indian Spice)

Warms up your heart.

Yield: serves 4

3   cups water

4   tablespoons coconut sugar or sweetener
    of your choice

5   cloves

1   stick cinnamon

1   tablespoon black tea leaves or 2 tea bags

2   cups soy/rice/nut milk

5   cardamom pods, crushed

5   black peppercorns, crushed

1   inch/2.5cm ginger, crushed

1. Boil water with spices. Add tea leaves and coconut sugar when boiled, lower the heat and simmer for a few minutes.
2. Add milk and warm on low heat. Strain to serve.

DIPS AND CRACKERS

As a snack, easy breakfast, appetizer, with wine, for a party—perfect for any occasion!

Golden Carrot Dip

I love this super simple, silky, creamy dip! It is so nutritious and easy to make. Perfect for babies! Wonderful with **Chapatti Chips** (see variation of **Tortilla de Chapatti** recipe on page 35).

Yield: 2-3 cups

1	lb/500g carrot, boiled or steamed until soft	3	tablespoons olive oil
1	teaspoon salt	1	teaspoon cumin powder
1	teaspoon caraway seeds (optional)	4	tablespoons water

1. Blend all ingredients in a blender until smooth. Add a little more water if necessary to facilitate easy blending.

Tahini Tofu Cheese

This goes well with **Savoury Oat Biscuits** (on page 37)!

Yield: about 2 cups

10	oz./300g firmed tofu (see **Firming Tofu** on page 22)		
4	tablespoons oil of your choice	3	tablespoons maple syrup
3	tablespoons tahini	2	tablespoons lemon juice
1	teaspoon salt		

1. Process all ingredients in the food processor until smooth.

Cashew Sour Cream

This recipe ensures you'll have no difficulty giving up dairy products!

Yield: 2 cups

2	cups cashew nuts, soaked in water for 2-4 hours, rinsed and drained		
4	tablespoons olive oil	4	tablespoons lemon juice
1	tablespoon apple cider vinegar	2	teaspoons salt
8	tablespoons water		

1. Blend all ingredients in a blender until smooth. Add a little more water if necessary to facilitate easy blending.

Tortilla de Chapatti

Indian flatbread, chapatti, made with freshly ground whole-meal flour makes a healthy tortilla!

Yield: 8-10 pieces

2   cups whole-meal wheat flour or spelt flour
1   teaspoon oil of your choice
     pinch of salt
²/₃-1 cup lukewarm water or as needed
     flour for rolling as needed

1. Place flour, oil, and salt in a bowl, gradually add water, and knead well for 3-5 minutes. The dough should be as soft as an earlobe. Add a little more water if it is too hard.
2. Cover with a wet towel and leave for a half hour at room temperature.
3. Make 8-10 small balls, dash a little additional flour on the rolling board, and roll out to a circle 6–8 inches/15-20cm in diameter.
4. Panfry without oil over low flame on both sides.
5. Keep warm, covered with dry towel, until it is ready to serve.

Variation:

Chapatti Chips

Often in my retreats, chapattis from the day before turn into healthy chips for the next day. Fabulous with any dip!

1. Cut Tortilla de Chapatti into 6-8 triangles.
2. Bake in the oven at 300 ° F/150 ° C for 15-20 minutes or until slightly brown and crispy.
3. If you don't have an oven, panfry without oil over lowest heat on both sides.

Savoury Oat Biscuits

These biscuits particularly go well with thick creamy dip. I like to use nutrient-rich ragi flour, Indian black millet, which adds a distinguished flavour. Try with any of your favourite flours, such as buckwheat, maize, millet, etc.

Yield: 21 biscuits

5 oz./150g rolled oats

1.8 oz./50g wheat flour or spelt flour

1.2 oz./35g flour of your choice (buckwheat, maize, millet)

1.4 oz./40g walnuts

½ teaspoon salt

2.6 oz. by volume/75ml oil of your choice

1 tablespoon maple syrup

1.4-1.8 oz. by volume/40-50ml water

flour for rolling, as needed

1. Preheat the oven to 350° F/180° C.
2. Process all the flours, oats, walnuts, and salt in the food processor into powder.
3. Slowly add the oil and maple syrup until the mixture resembles coarse breadcrumbs.
4. Keep pulsing and add water slowly. The mixture will immediately combine.
5. Transfer into a bowl and combine the mixture evenly by hand. Add a little more water if the dough is too hard to roll. (The quantity of water depends on the variety of flour.)
6. Roll it into an 6x8-inch/15x21cm square with additional flour on the board.
7. Place the parchment paper over the surface to stick to the dough, turn it over then cut into 2x2 inch/3x5cm each or any size you like.
8. Bake in the oven for about 20 minutes or until slightly brown.

SOUPS

Such a wonderful, hearty comfort food they are!

Thai Pumpkin Coconut Soup

The most popular item at my yoga retreats!

Yield: serves 4-6

2	tablespoons oil of your choice
1	clove garlic, minced
2	teaspoons cumin seeds
1	inch/2.5cm sliced galangal; if unavailable, use sliced ginger
2	stalks lemon grass root, bruised
4	kaffir lime leaves
1	small onion, sliced
21	oz./600g pumpkin, cut into big chunks
1	teaspoon salt or to taste
2	tablespoons soy sauce or tamari
¼	teaspoon chilli powder
2-3	cups water
1½	cups coconut milk

FYI: If vegetarian green curry paste is available, you can substitute all the spices (cumin seeds, galangal, lemon grass, kaffier lime leaves, and chilli powder) with 1/2-1 tablespoon green curry paste, which makes it so easy to prepare.

Garnish:

2-3 tablespoons coconut cream (optional)

1. In a soup pot, sauté garlic, cumin seeds, galangal, lemon grass root, and kaffir lime leaves in the oil.
2. Add the onion and salt, lower the heat and let it simmer for a while until the onion turns slightly brown.
3. Add pumpkin and sauté for 5 minutes.
4. Add water, soy sauce, and chilli powder and bring to a boil over medium heat.
5. Reduce to low heat and cook pumpkin until soft.
6. Take out and discard lemon grass and kaffier lime leaves, blend into puree with coconut milk, using blender or hand blender. (If you are using a blender, cool it down a little bit before blending.)
7. Warm it up again to serve if necessary.
8. Garnish with coconut cream if desired.

Beetroot Cleansing Soup

Super simple, yet very nourishing.

Yield: serves 4-6

2	tablespoons oil of your choice
1	teaspoon mustard seeds
1	clove garlic, minced (optional)
2	teaspoons cumin seeds
10	curry leaves; if unavailable, omit or use ½ teaspoon curry powder
1	onion, chopped
21	oz./600g beetroot, peeled and sliced
2	teaspoons salt or to taste
3-4	cups water

FYI: Curry leaves are the leaves of the curry trees used in Southeast Asian cooking. They give a very distinct flavour and aroma to dishes. Although they are not related to curry powder at all, if it is difficult to find them, either omit or add some curry powder to create an exotic flavour.

Garnish:

2-3 tablespoons **Cashew Sour Cream** (see **Dips and Crackers** on page 33) (optional)

1. In a soup pot, heat the mustard seeds in the oil.
2. When they start popping, add the garlic and cumin seeds, and then the curry leaves. (If using curry powder, add it later, as it burns easily.)
3. Immediately add the onion and salt, lower the heat, and let it simmer for a while until the onion turns slightly brown.
4. Add beetroot and sauté for 3-5 minutes.
5. Add water, bring to a boil, lower the heat and cook beetroot, covered, until soft.
6. Blend into puree, using a blender or hand blender. (If you are using a blender, cool it down a little bit before blending.)
7. Warm it up again to serve if necessary.
8. Garnish with cashew sour cream if desired.

Variation: Pure Veggie Soup

Simply replace beetroot with your favourite vegetables such as carrot, pumpkin, sweet potato, potato, or leek and try your favourite different spices and herbs.

Healing Miso Soup

Medicinal tea in the miso soup! Try with any of your favourite medicinal teas! My favourite is black bean tea, which makes miso soup mild and slightly sweet.

Yield: serves 4

6 cups water

4 tablespoons or 4-5 teabag medicinal tea of your choice

5-7 tablespoons miso of your choice or to taste

2 teaspoons kelp powder

3.5 oz./100g tofu, cut into cubes

1 handful chopped green onion

1-2 tablespoons dry wakame or 1 handful fresh wakame

1. Bring the water to a boil with the medicinal tea. (Cook longer if necessary according to the directions of the tea.)
2. Turn the heat off and strain or take out the tea bag.
3. Dissolve the miso and kelp powder completely.
4. Add the rest of the ingredients and serve.

Dal Soup

This was my first introduction to Ayurvedic cooking. So simple, soooooo tasty and nourishing! This seasoning is the basic in South Indian and Ayurvedic dishes. It helps digestion and balances all constitutions.

Yield: serves 4-6

1 cup yellow mung dal (split mung beans)

½ teaspoon turmeric powder

1 tablespoon oil of your choice

1 teaspoon cumin seeds

6 cups water

1 teaspoon salt or to taste

1 teaspoon mustard seeds

1 clove garlic, minced (optional)

10 curry leaves; if unavailable, use ½ teaspoon curry powder

1. Cook dal with water and turmeric powder until soft, then add salt and set aside.
2. In a pan, heat the mustard seeds in the oil.
3. When they start popping, add the cumin seeds, then the garlic and curry leaves. (If using curry powder, add it later as it burns easily.)
4. Immediately add to the dal and stir.
5. Simmer over a low flame for a few minutes.

Simplest Tomato Basil Soup

The key for this tasty vegan soup is to take time to sauté the vegetables over low heat to create the gentle energy in the soup.

Yield: serves 4-6

2	tablespoons oil of your choice	2	cloves garlic, minced
1	onion, finely chopped	1	carrot, finely chopped
½	stalk celery, finely chopped	1	teaspoon salt or to taste
1	teaspoon dry basil	2	cups water

3 cups fresh or canned tomatoes, blended into puree

2-3 tablespoons chopped fresh basil

1. In a soup pot, sauté the garlic and onion in the oil, sprinkle salt on top, and cook over low heat, covered, for 3-5 minutes or until soft.
2. Stir in carrot, celery, and dry basil and cook for another few minutes, covered, or until soft and slightly brown. Add tomato puree and water, and bring to a boil over medium heat.
3. Reduce to low heat and cook for another 15 minutes.
4. Turn off the heat and stir in chopped basil at the end.

Moroccan Spiced Chickpea Soup

This delicious, hearty North African stew is great with couscous or warm bread.

Yield: serves 4-6

2	tablespoons oil of your choice	2	cloves garlic, minced
1	tablespoon grated ginger	1	onion, diced
1	carrot, diced	2	potatoes, diced
1	cup cooked chickpeas (see the **Techniques chapter** on page 26 for how to cook)	1	teaspoon cumin powder
2-3	tablespoons raisins	1	teaspoon paprika powder
½	teaspoon cinnamon powder	1	tablespoon soy sauce or tamari
1	teaspoon salt or to taste	4	cups water

1. In a soup pot, sauté the garlic, ginger, and onion in the oil, sprinkle salt on top and cook, covered, over low heat for 3-5 minutes or until soft.
2. Stir in carrot and potato with all the spices and cook, covered, for another few minutes or until soft.
3. Add soy sauce, raisins, chickpeas, and water and bring to a boil over medium heat.
4. Reduce to low heat and cook for another 15 minutes.

Vietnamese "Pho" Noodle Soup

Its textures of broth and noodle, and its flavours of herbs and spices . . . what a wonderful interplay! This is why I love Southeast Asian food!

Yield: serves 4-6

3	tablespoons sesame oil or oil of your choice	1	clove garlic, sliced
1	tablespoon julienned ginger	1	onion, sliced
5	shitake mushrooms, sliced	1	stalk celery, sliced
½	bell pepper, julienned	2	cups shredded cabbage
10	whole cloves	4	whole star anises
1	cinnamon stick	3	tablespoons soy sauce or tamari
2	tablespoons coconut sugar or sweetener of your choice		
1	tablespoon lemon juice	1	teaspoon salt or to taste
4	cups water		

Garnish:

1.8 oz./50g rice noodles, soaked in boiled water for 5 minute or until soft, washed in cold water, and drained

2-3 tablespoons chopped cilantro (coriander leaf)

1-2 chopped fresh chilli (optional)

1. In a soup pot, sauté the garlic, ginger, and onion with all the spices in the oil.
2. Sprinkle salt on top and cook over low heat, covered, for 3-5 minutes or until soft and slightly brown.
3. Add mushroom, celery, bell pepper, cabbage, soy sauce, coconut sugar, and lemon juice and cook, covered, for another few minutes or until soft.
4. Add water and bring to a boil over medium heat.
5. Reduce to low heat and cook for another 15 minutes.
6. Add rice noodles before serving and garnish with cilantro and chilli if desired (if you like heat).

SALADS, DRESSINGS, AND ALMIGHTY SAUCES

These salads are too good to play just a side role. They should be treated as a main feature with all the delicious dressings and sprinkles!

Greek Salad with Tofu-Feta

How simple Mediterranean cuisine is! The combination of fresh veggies, tofu-feta, herbs, and refreshing lemon and olive oil makes it such a pleasant and perfect healthy meal.

Yield: serves 4

9	oz./250g firmed tofu (see **Firming Tofu** on page 22), cubed
1	head romaine lettuce, cut into bite-sized pieces
1-2	cucumbers, large diced
2-3	tomatoes, (deseeded and) large diced
1	bell pepper, round sliced
¼	red onion, thinly round sliced
20-30 olives	

Lemon Dressing:

(yield: 1 ¼ cups)

1	cup olive oil
4	tablespoons lemon juice
2	tablespoons chopped oregano or 2 teaspoons dry oregano
1	tablespoon salt
¼	teaspoon freshly cracked black pepper

1. For the lemon dressing, mix all ingredients in a bowl.
2. To make tofu-feta cheese, marinate tofu with 6 tablespoons lemon dressing and keep in the fridge for 1 hour.
3. To assemble, top romaine lettuce with all the vegetables, tofu-feta cheese and olives, and serve with lemon dressing.

Chinese Ban-Ban-Jee Salad

Ban-ban-jee is a Japanese-influenced Chinese salad. It usually comes with boiled chicken, but we serve it with teriyaki tofu!

Yield: serves 4

Teriyaki Tofu:

14 oz./400g firmed tofu (see **Firming Tofu** on page 22), sliced into halves

1 tablespoon sesame oil	1 tablespoon soy sauce or tamari
1 head iceberg lettuce, shredded	1-2 cups julienned cucumber
1-2 cups julienned carrot	1-2 cups (deseeded and) thinly sliced tomato

Garnish:

2-3 tablespoons chopped chive

1 tablespoon black sesame seeds

Ban-Ban-Jee Dressing

(yield: 1½ cups)

½ cup tahini

4½ tablespoons sesame oil

2 tablespoons grated ginger

2 tablespoons rice vinegar or vinegar of your choice

1½ tablespoons coconut sugar or sweetener of your choice

1½ tablespoons Dijon mustard

1½ tablespoons soy sauce or tamari

3/4 teaspoon salt or to taste

6 tablespoons water

1. For the ban-ban-jee dressing, blend all ingredients in a blender until smooth.
2. For the teriyaki tofu, panfry the tofu in the sesame oil on both sides until lightly brown.
3. Drizzle soy sauce and cook for a few seconds. Soy sauce is easy to burn so turn the heat off after the aroma is released to avoid burning. Slice into bite-sized pieces.
4. To assemble, spread iceberg lettuce on the plate, arrange the cucumber, carrot, and tomatoes on top, place sliced teriyaki tofu in the middle and garnish with chive and black sesame seeds.
5. Serve with the ban-ban-jee dressing on the side

Warm Quinoa and Roasted Vegetable Salad

Quinoa is a wonderful, healthy food, has more protein than rice and other grains, and is also a great source of fiber and minerals. It is great with some sprinkles of nuts and dry fruits!

Yield: serves 4

2   cups cooked quinoa (see **Techniques** on page 24 for how to cook quinoa)
¼   cup basil, julienned

Roasted Vegetables:

4-5 asparagus, cut into 2 inch/5cm lengths
2   bell peppers, large chunked
2   zucchini, large chunked
1   eggplant, large chunked
1   onion, large chunked

Balsamic Vinaigrette: (yield: 1 cup)

8   tablespoons olive oil
6   tablespoons balsamic vinegar
2   tablespoons maple syrup or sweetener of your choice
1   teaspoon salt
     pinch of black pepper

Garnish:

1   cup **Tofu-Ricotta Cheese** (see page 89) (optional)

1. For the balsamic vinaigrette, mix all ingredients in a bowl.
2. Preheat oven to 400 ° F/200 ° C. Lightly grease a baking sheet or line with parchment paper.
3. Place all ingredients for roasted vegetables in a large bowl and toss with the balsamic vinaigrette, saving some for finishing.
4. Spread tossed vegetables onto the baking sheet, roast in the oven for about 15 minutes or until soft and golden brown. If you don't have an oven, panfry over low heat.
5. Place quinoa, roasted vegetables, and basil in a bowl and toss with the rest of balsamic vinaigrette.
6. Garnish with a sprinkle of tofu-ricotta cheese if desired.

Zen Soba Noodle Salad

Soba, meaning buckwheat in Japanese, has a cooling property and is popular in the hot and humid summers in Japan. It also helps to get rid of water retention in our bodies.

Yield: serves 4

6	oz./180g dry soba noodles
2	cups frozen or fresh edamame beans (young soy beans in the pod)
4	cups shredded lettuce of any kind
1½	cups julienned carrots
1½	cups julienned daikon radish

Soba Noodle Dressing: (yield: ¾ cup)

3	tablespoons sesame oil
3	tablespoons rice vinegar or vinegar of your choice
3	tablespoons soy sauce or tamari
3	tablespoons coconut sugar syrup or sweetener of your choice
1	tablespoon tahini

Garnish:

2	tablespoons chopped chives
2	tablespoons ground sesame seeds
¼	nori sheet, shredded

1. For the soba noodle dressing, mix all ingredients in a bowl.
2. Cook edamame beans in boiled water with some salt for 5 minutes or until beans are soft; drain, let it cool down, and then squeeze the pods with fingers to press the beans out.
3. Bring a pot of water to a boil. Add the soba and cook until "al dente," to be firm but not hard.
4. Once cooked, rinse under cold water until cool, then drain.
5. Place all the vegetables in a bowl, then arrange soba noodles in the middle, top with edamame beans, and pour the dressing on top.
6. Garnish with chives, sesame seed, and nori.

Balinese Gado-Gado Salad
(Steamed Veggies with Peanut Butter Sauce)

Classic Balinese cuisine! Its sweet peanut butter flavour and unique tempeh combination is quite addictive!

Yield: serves 4

2	cups each bean shoots (bean sprouts), potato, broccoli, and carrot, or any veggies of your choice
4	oz./125g tempeh, thinly sliced
1½	tablespoons sesame oil or oil of your choice
1½	teaspoons soy sauce or tamari

Gado-Gado Sauce: (yield: 1½ cups)

2	cloves garlic, crushed
1	tablespoon grated ginger
1	cup chopped tomato
½	cup peanut butter
3	tablespoons soy sauce or tamari
3	tablespoons coconut sugar or sweetener of your choice
1	tablespoon lemon juice
2	teaspoons onion powder
1	teaspoon cumin powder
½	teaspoon chilli powder
½	teaspoon salt or to taste

Garnish:

4   tablespoons **Crispy Shallot** (see **Fun Salad Sprinkles** on page 63) (optional)

1. For the gado-gado sauce, blend all ingredients in a blender until smooth. Add a little more tomato or water if necessary to facilitate easy blending.
2. Cut the veggies of your choice into bite-sized pieces, steam or boil them, and set aside.
3. For the tempeh, panfry the tempeh in the oil on both sides until lightly brown, drizzle soy sauce and cook for a few seconds. Soy sauce is easy to burn so turn the heat off after the aroma is released to avoid burning.
4. Arrange the vegetables and tempeh on a plate, serve with the gado-gado sauce on the side, and sprinkle crispy shallots on top if desired.

Fig and Balsamic Dressing

Fig and balsamic: this classic marriage is such a golden combination. 1+1 makes much more than 2!

Yield: 1¼ cup

4   tablespoons chopped dried figs, soaked in minimum water for 30 minutes
3   tablespoons olive oil
3   tablespoons balsamic vinegar
½   teaspoon white miso
½   teaspoon salt
    pinch of black pepper
½   teaspoon each thyme and rosemary (or ¼ teaspoon dry each)
6   tablespoons water (or fig soaking water if you like it sweeter

1.   Blend all ingredients in the blender except for thyme and rosemary.
2.   Add thyme and rosemary and blend for a few seconds.

Japanese Dressing

Sweet, salty, and sour: that's the basic composition of "Japanese" flavour. Never goes wrong. Not only for salad, it is great for steamed veggies, tofu, and rice salad!

Yield: 1 cup

4   tablespoons sesame oil
4   tablespoons rice vinegar or vinegar of your choice
4   tablespoons soy sauce or tamari
4   tablespoons coconut sugar syrup or sweetener of your choice
2   tablespoons ground white sesame seeds

1. Mix all ingredients in a bowl.

French Dressing

Oil-to-vinegar = 3:1. This is the golden ratio of basic dressing. You can arrange the other component, such as herbs and spices, and make your original dressing!

Yield: 1½ cups

1	cup olive oil
⅓	cup (or 6 tablespoons) white wine vinegar or vinegar of your choice
2	tablespoons chopped onion
1	tablespoon lemon juice
1	teaspoon Dijon mustard
1	teaspoon salt
	pinch of black pepper

1. Blend all ingredients in a blender until well incorporated.

Italian Vinaigrette

This is a staple in my kitchen. It's great to marinate veggies with as well!

Yield: 1 cup

½	cup olive oil
½	cup apple cider vinegar or vinegar of your choice
3	tablespoons maple syrup or sweetener of your choice
1½	teaspoons salt
½	teaspoon Italian dry mix herb
	pinch of black pepper

1. Mix all ingredients in a bowl.

Variation: Orange Fennel Salad

Marinate thinly sliced fennel bulbs and segmented oranges with Italian vinaigrette.

Tahina Sauce

Not to mention this goes well with **Falafels** (see page 83), it can be served with any steamed veggies or fresh salad!

Yield: 1 cup

- $1/3$ cup (6 tablespoons) tahini
- 2 tablespoons lemon juice
- 1 tablespoon olive oil
- $1/2$ tablespoon soy sauce or tamari
- $1/2$ teaspoon salt or to taste
- $1/2$ teaspoon cumin powder
- $1/3$ cup (6 tablespoons) water

1. Blend all ingredients in a blender until smooth or mix in a bowl.

Cashew Mayonnaise

This can be kept in the fridge for 1 week or more. Say goodbye to the commercial mayonnaise made out of all that we cannot even recognise!

Yield: 2 cups

- 2 cups cashew nuts, soaked
- 4 tablespoons olive oil
- 2 tablespoons apple cider vinegar
- $1\frac{1}{2}$ teaspoons salt
- $1/2$ cup water

1. Blend all ingredients in a blender until smooth.

Raw Ketchup

Commercial ketchup is full of white sugar and refined salt. Delicious homemade ketchup is super easy, so why not keep it as a staple? It can be kept in the fridge for 1 week or more.

Yield: 2 cups

1	cup dried tomato, soaked in water for 30 minutes
¾	cup chopped tomato
5	tablespoons chopped dates
4	tablespoons apple cider vinegar or vinegar of your choice
1	teaspoon salt

1. Blend all ingredients in a blender until well incorporated. Add a little more tomato or water if necessary to facilitate easy blending.

Rita's Coconut Chutney

Rita is like my lovely Indian mother. She makes the best chutney! It makes a great accompaniment to any Indian dishes, and is especially great with chapatti.

Yield: 1½ cups

1½	cups freshly grated mature coconut; if unavailable, use dry coconut
½	cup chopped cilantro (coriander) (including stem and root)
2	fresh green chillies, deseeded, or to taste
8-10	curry leaves; if unavailable, omit
1	tablespoon grated ginger
1	clove garlic, crushed
2	tablespoons lemon juice
2	teaspoons coconut sugar or sweetener of your choice
1	teaspoon salt or to taste
4-8	tablespoons water or as needed (depending on the dryness of coconut)

1. Blend all ingredients in a blender until well incorporated. Add a little more water if necessary to facilitate easy blending.

FUN SALAD SPRINKLES

Magic sprinkles to make
the ordinary salad
delicious and exciting!

Gomashio

This is a staple for macrobiotic dishes. Great on top of rice, salad, or anything!

Yield: 2 cups

2　cups black or white sesame seeds
1　teaspoon salt or to taste (more or less, according to your needs)

1. Place sesame seeds and salt in a pan, dry roast over a low flame until slightly brown.
2. Make into powder using a pestle and mortar, grinder, or blender.

Thai Peanuts

Nice on top of salad or as a snack!

Yield: 2 cups

1　tablespoon oil of your choice
2　inches/5cm stalk lemon grass root, finely chopped
6-8 kaffir lime leaves, thinly sliced
1　clove garlic, thinly sliced
1　teaspoon chopped fresh chilli or ½ teaspoon chilli flakes
2　cups roasted peanuts
1　tablespoon maple syrup
1　teaspoon cumin seeds
2　tablespoons chopped green onion
1　tablespoon soy sauce or tamari
½　teaspoon salt

1. Panfry the ingredients in order from the top of the list.

South Indian Cashews

Another variation of nut and seed snacks! Play around with the herbs and spices and make your original salad sprinkle! The variations are infinite.

Yield: 2 cups

1　tablespoon oil of your choice
1　teaspoon cumin seeds
8-10 curry leaves; if unavailable, use ½ teaspoon curry powder
1　teaspoon salt
1 tablespoon maple syrup
1　teaspoon mustard seeds
2　cups cashew nuts
1　teaspoon curry powder
3　tablespoons raisins

1. Panfry the ingredients in order from the top of the list.

Cashew Nut "Parmesan"

This is an instant cheesy-nut topping for Italian dishes. I love to sprinkle this on top of salad!

Yield: 1 cup

1   cup cashew nuts
1   tablespoon nutritional yeast
1   tablespoon smoked paprika powder; if unavailable, use normal paprika powder
1   teaspoon salt

1. Process all ingredients in the food processor into powder.

Brazilian Nut "Parmesan"

Inspired by my favourite recipe book "I am grateful" —tastes absolutely gorgeous!

Yield: 1 cup

1   cup Brazilian nuts
1   tablespoon nutritional yeast
1   clove garlic, minced
1   teaspoon salt

1. Process all ingredients in the food processor until crumbled.

Crispy Shallot or Onion

Infinite usage! For salads, sandwiches, burgers, or as a spice for Asian dishes such as noodles and stir-fry veggies. Great even in mushed potato and teppanyaki!

Yield: 1½ cups

1½ cups shallots or onion, thinly sliced
4   tablespoons oil of your choice
½   teaspoon salt

1. Heat the oil in a pan over lowest heat. Add the shallot and sauté for 10-15 minutes or until brown without burning, stirring often.
2. Remove the shallots from the pan, sprinkle salt, and then set aside on a paper towel.
3. As they cool, they will crisp up.

SIDE DISHES

**Easy hit menus for snacks
and main dishes!**

Vietnamese Spring Rolls with Sweet Chilli Dipping Sauce

The number-one most popular Asian healthy dish! Makes us feel good and light, and satisfying with fresh herbs and lots of veggies.

Yield: 12 pieces

12 round 8.5 inch/22cm-sized rice paper sheets	2 oz./60g glass noodles
1 tablespoon soy sauce or tamari	1-2 cucumbers, julienned
1 carrot, julienned	2 avocados, sliced

½ cup Asian herbs such as cilantro (coriander leaf), basil or mint

½ cup roasted peanuts, crushed

Serving:

Sweet Chilli Sauce (see below) as needed

1. Soak glass noodles in boiled water for 3-5 minutes or until soft, wash in cold water, drain well, cut into 2 inch/5cm-pieces, and mix soy sauce.
2. Prepare water in a large bowl. Dip the rice paper (one or two at once) into the water for a few seconds (or follow the directions on the package for duration) and place on a clean flat surface.
3. On the rice paper, about 1.5 inches/4cm from the bottom edge, place some Asian herbs followed by the cucumber, carrot, avocado, and the glass noodles in the centre.
4. Carefully fold each side flap and roll away from you. Tuck all the mixture into the wrapper, forming a cigar. Serve with sweet chilli dipping sauce.

Sweet Chilli Dipping Sauce

Sometimes we take it for granted that this kind of sauce is something that we must buy at the supermarket, but indeed it is so simple to make at home!

Yield: ½ cup

6 tablespoons coconut sugar or sweetener of your choice	1 teaspoon chilli flakes
6 tablespoons rice vinegar or vinegar of your choice	½ teaspoon salt

½ cup water

½ teaspoons Kudzu (arrowroot powder), dissolved in 1 tablespoon water

1. Place all ingredients in a pot except for Kudzu mixture.
2. Bring to a boil, stirring occasionally; cook to reduce the liquid to half volume over a low flame.
3. Add arrowroot mixture and stir until the sauce becomes slightly thick in consistency

Indian Chickpea Snack

Mustard seeds, cumin seeds, garlic, and curry leaves: this South Indian flavour profile is my favourite! It makes the simple ingredients so flavourful and distinguished.

Yield: serves 4 as side meal or 2 as main meal

2   tablespoons oil of your choice

1   teaspoon mustard seeds

1   teaspoon cumin seeds

1   clove garlic, minced

30   curry leaves; if unavailable, use 1 teaspoon curry powder

1-2 fresh chillies, deseeded and chopped, or to taste

4   cups cooked chickpeas (see **Techniques** on page 26 for cooking chickpeas)

1   teaspoon salt or to taste

½   cup freshly grated mature coconut; if unavailable, use ground dry coconut

4   tablespoons chopped cilantro (coriander leaf)

1. In a sauté pan, heat the mustard seeds in the oil.
2. When they start popping, add cumin seeds and garlic, and then curry leaves and red chilli at the end. (If using curry powder, add it later as it burns easily.)
3. Immediately transfer into the bowl of chickpeas and toss with salt.
4. Fold in grated coconut and cilantro.

Tempeh Ginger Miso Sauté

Its sweet and rich miso flavour goes so well with simple rice or Asian noodles!

Yield: serves 4 as side meal or 2 as main meal

4   tablespoons sesame oil or oil of your choice
1   tablespoon soy sauce or tamari
11   oz./300g tempeh, thinly sliced
21   oz./600g green beans, cut into half lengthwise and lightly blanched

Miso Sauce:

3½   tablespoons dark miso
2½   tablespoons coconut sugar syrup or sweetener of your choice
2   tablespoons soy sauce or tamari
1   tablespoon grated ginger
1   teaspoon vinegar of your choice
2   tablespoons water

1. For the miso sauce, mix all ingredients in a bowl until miso is well dissolved.
2. Panfry tempeh in the sesame oil on both sides until lightly brown.
3. Drizzle soy sauce and cook for a few seconds.
4. Add miso sauce and stir well over medium heat for a few minutes.
5. Stir in green beans and mix well.

Tofu Pizza

New inspiration for tofu! This is my all-time hit at the yoga retreats. Enjoy with any sauces and vegetables you like!

Yield: serves 4 as side meal or 2 as main meal

28   oz./800g firmed tofu, 0.4inch/1cm sliced (see **Firming Tofu** <u>on page 22</u>)

2   cups **Marinara Sauce** (<u>see page 101</u>)

½   cup **Cashew Cheese Sauce** (<u>see page 110</u>)

2-3   tablespoons **Cashew or Brazilian Nut "Parmesan"** (<u>see page 63</u>)

Pizza Toppings:

1   bell pepper, diced, or any vegetables of your choice

1 ½   cups mushroom of any kind, diced

1-2   tablespoons fresh herbs of your choice

2-3   tablespoons olives, deseeded and sliced

1. Preheat the oven to 350° F/180° C. Lightly grease a baking sheet or line with parchment paper.
2. Place tofu onto the baking tray, then spread marinara sauce on top.
3. Top with all the pizza toppings.
4. Squeeze cashew cheese sauce to decorate.
5. Sprinkle "parmesan" on top.
6. Bake for about 10-20 minutes or until slightly brown on top.

SANDWICHES AND BURGERS

Veggie burgers are the most popular dishes at my retreats!

Tofu Burgers

The secret for nice and rich burgers is to drain the water well from the tofu and to sauté the vegetables well until sweet!

Yield: 8 burgers

4 tablespoons oil of your choice	1 clove garlic, minced
½ teaspoon cumin seeds	1 onion, finely chopped
½ carrot, finely chopped	¼ stalk celery, finely chopped
1 teaspoon salt or to taste	¼ teaspoon black pepper
½ teaspoon nutmeg powder	1 tablespoon tahini

14 oz./400g firmed tofu, crumbled by hand (see Firming Tofu in Techniques chapter)

3.5 oz./100g any cooked beans or roasted nuts, chopped

1 tablespoon soy sauce or tamari	5 tablespoons flour of your choice

Serving:

8 pieces whole meal burger buns

Cashew Mayonnaise, as needed (see page 58)

Raw Ketchup, as needed (see page 59)

Mustard, as needed

Lettuce, tomato and avocado, as needed

1. Sauté the garlic and cumin in the oil over medium heat.
2. Add the onion, carrot, and celery and sprinkle salt, black pepper, and nutmeg powder on top and cook, covered, over low heat for 3-5 minutes or until soft.
3. Transfer into a bowl and let cool down.
4. Add the rest of ingredients except for the flour and mix by hand.
5. Add flour and mix until well incorporated. Add more flour if the mixture is too soft to form the patties.
6. Form into burger-sized patties (about 3 inches/7.5cm in diameter) and panfry in some additional oil on both sides until lightly brown.
7. To assemble, spread cashew mayonnaise and mustard onto the burger buns, spread lettuce, tomato, and avocado, place tofu burger, pour the raw ketchup, and cover with the buns.

Variation:
Japanese-Style Rice Bowl with Teriyaki Ginger Sauce

Make **Teriyaki Ginger Sauce** (see below) in a pan and dip the burgers in the sauce. Place cooked rice in a big bowl, top with burger and pour on more sauce. Garnish with chopped chives on top if desired.

Teriyaki Ginger Sauce

This popular Japanese sauce is great for sautéed vegetables, tofu, and tempeh.

Yield: 3/4 cup

- 8   tablespoons soy sauce or tamari
- 2   tablespoons maple syrup or sweetener of your choice
- 1   tablespoon grated ginger
- 8   tablespoons water
- 1   teaspoon Kudzu (arrowroot powder) dissolved in 8 tablespoons water

1. Place all ingredients in a pot except for Kudzu mixture.

2. Bring to a boil, stirring; cook to reduce the liquid to half volume over a low flame.

3. Add Kudzu mixture, and stir until the sauce becomes slightly thick in consistency.

Tempeh Burgers

Tempeh is the best meat substitute for someone in the transitional stage of becoming a vegetarian. It is fermented soybeans, originated in Indonesia and its "stinky" aroma is quite addictive!

Yield: 8-10 burgers

2	tablespoons oil of your choice
1	clove garlic, minced
½	teaspoon cumin seeds
1	onion, finely chopped
½	carrot, finely chopped
¼	stalk celery, finely chopped
1	teaspoon salt or to taste
¼	teaspoon black pepper
16	oz./450g tempeh, mashed by hand or in the food processor
2	tablespoons chopped basil or 2 teaspoons dry basil
1	tablespoon maple syrup or sweetener of your choice
1	tablespoon tahini
1	tablespoon soy sauce or tamari
1	tablespoon lemon juice
1	teaspoon Dijon mustard
½	teaspoon cumin powder
	(flour of your choice as needed, if necessary, to form patties)

1. Sauté the garlic and cumin seeds in the oil over medium heat.
2. Add the onion, carrot, and celery, and sprinkle salt and black pepper on top and cook, covered, over low heat for 3-5 minutes or until soft.
3. Transfer into a bowl and let it cool down.
4. Add all the rest of ingredients and mix well. Add some flour if the mixture is too soft to form patties.
5. Form into burger-sized patties (about 3 inches/7.5cm in diameter) and panfry in some additional oil on both sides until lightly brown.

Thai Corn-and-Peanut Burger Patties with Sweet Chilli Sauce

This is an Asian variation of a falafel! Easy to prepare and tastes wow! Surprise your friends!

Yield: 10-12 burgers

1½	cups fresh or frozen corn kernel (thawed if frozen)
1½	cups peanuts
2	tablespoons chopped basil
1	tablespoon soy sauce or tamari
1	tablespoon lemon juice
1	teaspoon coconut sugar or sweetener of your choice
½	teaspoon salt
½	teaspoon black pepper
¼	teaspoon chilli powder
½	cup potato starch or tapioca flour

Serving:

Sweet Chilli Dipping Sauce (see **Side Dishes** chapter on page 65)

1. Process corn and peanuts in the food processor until well ground.
2. Add all the rest of the ingredients, except for potato starch, and process evenly.
3. Transfer the mixture into a bowl and mix potato starch in by hand until well incorporated.
4. Form into small patties (about 2 inches/5cm in diameter) and panfry in some additional oil on both sides until lightly brown.
5. Serve with sweet chilli dipping sauce.

Wraps and Tortilla Dishes

Wraps are fun to fill, fold, and bite!!

Mexican Burrito

You can roll anything you like, such as fried rice and sautéed vegetables. This is the most popular burrito at the retreats! People love having it and learning how easy it is to prepare at home!

Yield: as much as you like

Tortilla de Chapatti (see page 35)

Chilli Beans (see page 80) or **Raw Taco Meat** (see page 80)

Cashew Sour Cream (see page 33)

Pineapple Salsa (see page 81)

Guacamole (see page 81)

1. Spoon about ½ cup chilli beans or raw taco meat and 2 tablespoons of cashew sour cream onto each tortilla just below the centre, loading on only as much filling as the tortilla can hold and still be folded and rolled.
2. Fold the bottom edge up and over the filling, (and then fold the both sides in if the tortilla is big enough) and over the filling. Roll up the burrito from the bottom.
3. Cut burrito in half on a bias if desired.
4. Serve with pineapple salsa and guacamole.

Variation: Try other variations of Mexican dishes!

Taco/tostada: Prepare tortilla de chapatti, baked in the oven. Top with shredded lettuce, chilli beans, or raw taco meat, salsa and guacamole, and pour cashew sour cream over the top.

Enchilada: Make burritos, pour some cashew sour cream on top, bake in the oven, and serve with guacamole and salsa.

Chilli Beans

Exotic spicy beans are ready in no time! Simply great on top of bread, or as a spread mushed into a paste, or you can cook with more water to make soup—many variations!

Yield: 5 cups

3 cups cooked kidney beans (see **Techniques** on page 26 for cooking beans)

4 tablespoons olive oil or oil of your choice

1 clove garlic, minced	1 onion, finely chopped
½ carrot, finely chopped	½ stalk celery, finely chopped
2 tablespoons cumin powder	1 tablespoon paprika powder
1 tablespoon dry oregano	1 teaspoon chilli powder or to taste
2 teaspoons salt	1 cup water

1. Sauté the garlic and onion in the oil, sprinkle salt on top and cook, covered, over low heat for 3-5 minutes or until soft.
2. Stir in carrot and celery with all the spices and cook, covered, for another few minutes or until soft.
3. Add kidney beans and water and bring to boil over medium heat.
4. Reduce to low heat and cook for another 10 minutes or until liquid is absorbed.

Raw Taco Meat

You won't believe it's raw! Walnuts mimic the meat texture and dark miso deepens the flavour. Delicious taco spiced with Mexican flavour!

Yield: 2 cups

2 cups walnuts, soaked in water for 8-12 hours, rinsed and drained

3 tablespoons sun-dried tomato, soaked in water for 30 minutes and minced

1 clove garlic, minced	2 tablespoons olive oil
2 tablespoons dark miso	2 teaspoons onion powder
2 teaspoons cumin powder	¼ teaspoon smoked salt

1 teaspoon smoked paprika powder; if unavailable, use normal paprika powder

1. In the food processor, pulse walnuts with the rest of the ingredients until crumbled. Scrape down the ingredients rising up around the edges in between pulsing to make them evenly processed. Add a little water if necessary to facilitate easy processing.

Pineapple Salsa

The tropical flavours of pineapple, lime, and cilantro (coriander leaf) make any main dishes light and fresh!

Yield: 3-4 cups

2	cups deseeded and small-diced tomato
1	cup small-diced pineapple
2	tablespoons minced red onion
2	tablespoons chopped cilantro (coriander leaf)
1-2	cloves garlic, minced
¼-½	jalapenos or fresh chilli, deseeded and minced, or to taste
3-4	tablespoons lime juice or to taste
	salt to taste
	black pepper to taste

1. Mix all ingredients in a bowl.

Guacamole

Everybody's favourite! Great for bread and crackers as well!

Yield: 3-4 cups

2	avocados
1	tomato, deseeded and small-diced
¼-½	jalapenos or fresh chilli, deseeded and minced, or to taste
2	tablespoons cilantro (coriander leaf), chopped
1	clove garlic, minced
1-2	tablespoons lime juice or to taste
1	teaspoon onion powder
½	teaspoon salt or to taste

1. Mash avocado in a bowl.
2. Add all the rest of the ingredients and mix well.

Mediterranean Mezzo

Falafel, babaganoush, and hummus with all the exotic sauces . . . it's a "must" menu item at the retreats! Make lots and share with your loved ones!

Yield: as much as you like

Tortilla de Chapatti (see page 35)
Falafel (see below)
Babaganoush (see page 84)
Hummus (see page 85)
Tahina Sauce (see page 58)
Tapenade (see page 85)
Tabouli de Couscous (see page 87)

1. Make a plate with all the items or roll your favourite filling with tortilla de chapatti like a burrito!

Falafel

Falafel originated in the Middle East and now you can find it everywhere in healthy vegan eateries! It is delicious with **Tahina Sauce** (see page 58) or **Hummus** (see page 85)!

Yield: 22 pieces

7   oz./200g uncooked dry chickpeas, soaked in plenty of water overnight, rinsed and drained
2   onions, chopped
2   cloves garlic, crushed
1   tablespoon chopped parsley or cilantro (coriander leaf)
2   teaspoons coriander seed powder
2   teaspoons cumin powder
     pinch of cayenne pepper or chilli powder
1½   teaspoons salt or to taste
     black pepper to taste
10   tablespoons chickpea flour or as needed; if unavailable, use wheat or spelt flour

1. Process all ingredients except for chickpea flour in the food processor into a pate.
2. Transfer into a bowl and mix in chickpea flour. Add some more flour if the mixture is too soft to form the patties.
3. Form 1.2 inches/3cm small balls or small flat patties and panfry on both sides in low heat with a generous amount of additional oil of your choice until golden brown.

Babaganoush

It's a grilled eggplant paste with tahini and spices similar to hummus. It goes well with pita bread and tortillas as well as crispy baguettes or toast!

Yield: 2 cups

2	large Italian eggplants
2	cloves garlic, crushed
2	tablespoons chopped parsley
4	tablespoons tahini
2	tablespoons olive oil
2	tablespoons lemon juice
1	teaspoon salt or to taste
1	teaspoon cumin powder
½	teaspoon black pepper

FYI: You can use a gas stove or grill to roast eggplant. Roast it over a medium flame until the skin becomes charred.

1. Preheat oven to 400 ° F/200 ° C. Lightly grease a baking sheet or line with parchment paper.
2. Place eggplants on the baking sheet and make holes in the skin with a fork. Roast for 30-40 minutes or until soft, turning occasionally. Remove from the oven, let cool slightly, peel off and discard the skin, and then transfer into the food processor.
3. Process eggplants with all the rest of the ingredients in the food processor until smooth.

Hummus

World-famous vegan dip!

Yield: 2 cups

1½   cups cooked chickpeas (see **Techniques** <u>on page 26</u> for how to cook chickpeas)
2   cloves garlic, crushed
⅓   cup (or 6 tablespoons) tahini
2   tablespoons olive oil
1   tablespoon lemon juice
1   teaspoon soy sauce or tamari
1   tablespoon cumin powder
¼   teaspoon black pepper
1   teaspoon salt or to taste
½   cup water (from cooking chickpea) or as needed

Garnish:

A dash olive oil, paprika powder, black pepper, or cumin powder

1. Process all ingredients in the food processor until smooth.
2. Garnish with olive oil and spices.

Tapenade

Classic Mediterranean olive paste. Great with bread and veggie sticks, as well as a pizza sauce and pasta sauce! So easy to make and lasts long! It can be kept in the fridge for 1 month or more.

Yield: 3/4 cup

1   cup olives, deseeded
1   tablespoon olive oil
1   tablespoon chopped parsley

1. Process all ingredients in a food processor until smooth.

Tabouli de Couscous

Tabouli (or tabbouleh or tabouleh) was a parsley salad with bulgur originally. Now I make it with couscous, easy to find and easy to cook. You can also make this salad with leftover rice! Loads of parsley, generous amount of olive oil, lemon and freshly ground black pepper makes it outstanding.

Yield: serves 4 as a side dish, 2 as a main dish

1	cup deseeded and small-diced tomato
1	cup small-diced cucumber
2	cups packed finely chopped parsley
2-3	tablespoons minced red onion
3	cloves garlic, minced
4	tablespoons olive oil
2	tablespoons lemon juice
1½	teaspoons freshly cracked black pepper
1½	teaspoons salt or to taste

Couscous:

½	cup couscous
1	tablespoon olive oil
½	cup boiling water

1. To prepare couscous, in a heat-proof bowl toss the couscous with 1 tablespoon olive oil.
2. Pour boiling water over it and place a lid or plastic wrap to seal completely and set aside.
3. After 5 minutes, uncover the couscous, and using a fork or by hand, separate the grains.
4. Let it cool to room temperature, then fold in the rest of the ingredients.

Italian Trico-Roll

Tortilla is an almighty bread that can be used in world dishes! Here I make it Italian with pesto, sun-dried tomatoes, and tofu-ricotta cheese. An elegant and colorful dish in a minute!

Yield: 6 rolls

6 sheets **Tortilla de Chapatti** (see page 35)

Filling:

1 ¼ cups **Fresh Basil Pesto Sauce**
(see page 110)

1 ½ cups **Marinated Sun-Dried Tomato**, sliced
(see page 89)

1 ½ cups **Tofu-Ricotta Cheese** (see page 89)

1 ½ cups arugula (rocket) or any dark greens
of your choice, cut into bite-sized pieces

1. Spread about 3 tablespoons of fresh basil pesto sauce onto the tortilla de chapatti.
2. Place about 4 tablespoons each of marinated sun-dried tomato, tofu-ricotta cheese, and arugula just below the centre.
3. Fold the bottom edge up and over the filling. Roll up tightly from the bottom. (It is a thinner roll than the burrito.)
4. Cut in half on a bias if desired.

Marinated Sun-Dried Tomato

This is the best way to enjoy its intense and concentrated flavour. With generous amounts of olive oil, garlic, and herbs, it becomes a wonderful appetizer. It can be kept in the fridge for 1 month or more.

Yield: 1½ cups

1½ cups sun-dried tomatoes, soaked in water for 30 minutes, well drained
¾ cup olive oil
2 cloves garlic, thinly sliced or minced
2 teaspoons Italian dry mixed herbs
   salt to taste (depending on the saltiness of sun-dried tomatoes)
   black pepper to taste

1. Marinate sun-dried tomatoes with the rest of the ingredients in a glass jar for more than 1 hour. The flavours come alive after 1 day of marinating.

Tofu-Ricotta Cheese

Super easy tofu cheese. Draining the tofu very well is the key to making it nice and rich.

Yield: 1½ cups

14 oz./400g firmed tofu (see **Firming Tofu** on page 22)
4 tablespoons olive oil
2 tablespoons lemon juice
2 tablespoons chopped basil
2 tablespoons nutritional yeast; if unavailable, use 1 tablespoon white miso
1½ teaspoons salt

1. In a bowl, crumble tofu by hand.
2. Add the rest of the ingredients and mix by hand.

Asian Peanut Miso Roll

Very easy to prepare and quite a unique dish! Another popular meal at the retreats! Sweet miso peanut butter never goes wrong!

Yield: 6 rolls

6   sheets **Tortilla de Chapatti** (see page 35)
1½   cups green beans
1½   cups carrots, cut into the same size as green beans
1½   cups **Teriyaki Tempeh** (see below)
1   cup **Peanut Miso Sauce** (see below)

1. Boil or steam green beans and carrots.
2. Spread 2½ tablespoons peanut miso sauce onto the tortilla de chapatti. Place some slices of teriyaki tempeh, ¼ cup each of carrots and green beans just below the centre.
3. Fold the bottom edge up and over the filling. Roll up tightly from the bottom.
4. Cut in half on a bias if desired.

Teriyaki Tempeh

The unique "stinky" flavour of tempeh can be reversed into addictively delicious by frying with flavourful sesame oil and finishing with soy sauce!

Yield: 2 cups

8   oz./225g tempeh, sliced into 0.4 inch/1cm pieces
2   tablespoons soy sauce or tamari   3   tablespoons sesame oil

1. Panfry tempeh in the oil on both sides until lightly brown. Drizzle soy sauce and cook for a few seconds. Soy sauce is easy to burn, so turn the heat off after the aroma is released to avoid burning.

Peanut Miso Sauce

Kids will love this sauce, not to mention adults!

Yield: 1 cup

3   tablespoons dark miso   3   tablespoons white miso
6   tablespoons peanut butter   3   tablespoons coconut sugar syrup or sweetener
     of your choice

1. Mix all ingredients in a bowl until smooth. Add a little water if necessary to smoothen

Snack Pizza

Super easy to make and light! Have fun playing around with your favourite pizza toppings!

Yield: 6 snack pizzas

6   sheets **Tortilla de Chapatti** (see page 35)

1-1½   cups **Marinara Sauce** (see page 101) or **Fresh Basil Pesto Sauce** (see page 110)

½   cup **Cashew Cheese Sauce** (see page 110)

3   cups any vegetable of your choice, cut into bite-sized pieces, fresh or sautéed

4   tablespoons olives, deseeded and sliced

2-3 tablespoons **Cashew or Brazilian Nuts "Parmesan"** (see page 63)

2-3 tablespoons fresh herbs of your choice

1. Preheat oven to 400 ° F/200 ° C. Lightly grease a baking sheet or line with parchment paper.
2. Spread 3-4 tablespoons marinara sauce or fresh basil pesto sauce onto each tortilla de chapatti.
3. Place about ½ cup vegetable of your choice on each, drop or squeeze some cashew cheese sauce and olives on top.
4. Bake for 10-15 minutes or until slightly brown on top.
5. Sprinkle with "parmesan" and herbs on each.

FUN WITH SUSHI AND MORE NORI ROLLS

Here is the good news . . . sushi doesn't mean raw fish!! So you can still enjoy sushi if you choose to be vegetarian or vegan or even a raw foodist!

You don't have to be a sushi expert. You can make your own easily and if you do, of course, it tastes phenomenonal!

Basic Sushi Roll

Is sushi something that you buy from the takeout shop? Making nori rolls at home is indeed quite simple. On top of that, if you make your own, it becomes a super special delicious roll no matter how it looks! Avocado plays the star role in vegetarian sushi, so use generously.

Yield: 4 thick rolls or 8 thin rolls

3   cups sushi rice (if using brown rice, soak overnight)

4   cups water or as needed (if using brown rice, need more water)

2   inches/5cm Kombu seaweed or 1 teaspoon kelp powder

2   avocados, sliced   2   cucumbers, julienned

1   carrot or bell pepper, julienned   4-8 sheets nori

Sushi Vinegar Mixture:

5   tablespoons rice vinegar or vinegar of your choice

3   tablespoons coconut sugar syrup or sweetener of your choice

1$^1/_3$ teaspoons salt

Serving:

soy sauce or tamari and wasabi paste

1. Cook rice with required water (see **Techniques** on page 24 for how to cook rice) with Kombu, or cook in a rice cooker (adjust the water required for the cooker).
2. When it is cooked, let it steam, covered, for 10-15 minutes, then take out the Kombu.
3. For the sushi vinegar mixture, mix all ingredients in a bowl until salt and sugar are well dissolved.
4. Transfer the rice into a large bowl and fold in the sushi vinegar mixture.
5. Cool it down immediately with a fan so that the rice absorbs the mixture and becomes shiny.
6. To assemble, place nori sheet over a bamboo mat. Wet your hands with water, take 1/4 amount of sushi rice for thick rolls (or 1/8 amount for thin rolls) and spread the rice evenly onto the nori sheet, leaving about 1 inch/2.5cm of nori empty at the top end. Arrange slices of cucumber, avocado and carrot or bell pepper across the centre of the rice. Lift the mat and roll over the vegetables and tuck it in under the filling. Moisten with a little water to help seal. Half unroll the mat then roll all over towards the exposed end of the nori sheet. Set aside and continue with remaining ingredients.
7. Using a sharp, wet knife, slice the rolls into 6-8 pieces. Dip the knife in water between slices so that each cut looks nice and clean.
8. Serve cut sides up and place soy sauce and wasabi paste on the side.

Tempeh Nori Rolls with No Rice

So easy! You don't even need a bamboo mat. I got this hint from teriyaki chicken sushi rolls overseas! As you can use any vegetables, it is, in a way, the best way to clean out your fridge and a really nice and handy snack or lunch!

Yield: as much as you like

> Spinach, arugula, shredded cabbage, or any leafy vegetables
>
> **Teriyaki Tempeh** (see page 91)
>
> Carrots, cucumbers, avocados julienned, or use any vegetables in the fridge!
>
> Nori sheets
>
> **Sesame Dipping Sauce** (see below)

1. Spread the leafy vegetables evenly onto the nori sheet, leaving about 1 inch/2.5cm of nori empty at the top end. Arrange slices of tempeh, carrot, cucumber, and avocado and drizzle of sesame dipping sauce across the centre of the leafy vegetables. Lift the edge of nori and roll over the filling and tuck it in under the filling. Moisten with a little bit of water or sesame dipping sauce to help seal. Then roll all the way towards the exposed end of the nori sheet. Then bite like burrito or slice into pieces like a proper sushi roll.

Sesame Dipping Sauce

This is a golden ratio of Japanese sweet, sour, and salty dipping sauce. So just remember the ratio NOW and you can make it any time, anywhere! Guaranteed your family and friends will rave about it! You can play around with flavour by adding some ginger, garlic, chilli, or chives.

Yield: 1/2 cup

3   tablespoons tahini

2   tablespoons soy sauce or tamari

2   tablespoons rice vinegar or vinegar of your choice

2   tablespoons coconut sugar syrup or sweetener of you choice

1. Mix all ingredients in a bowl.

Raw Un-Tuna Nori Roll

Now you know you can enjoy sushi rolls even if you choose to eat raw! Enjoy this unusual nori roll with Western-style tuna-like pate.

Yield: as much as you like

> Raw nori sheets
> Alfalfa sprouts
> Green leaves of your choice
> Sliced avocado or vegetable of your choice
> **Un-Tuna Raw Pate** (see below)

1. Spread alfalfa sprouts (just like placing rice) evenly onto the nori sheet, leaving about 1 inch/2.5cm of nori empty at the top end.
2. Arrange some green leaves, avocado and un-tuna raw pate across the centre of the alfalfa. Lift the edge of nori and roll over the filling and tuck it in under the filling. Moisten with a little water to help seal. Then roll all the way towards the exposed end of the nori sheet. Then bite like burrito or cut into pieces like a proper sushi roll.

Un-Tuna Raw Pate

This recipe was inspired by my dear friend Vanessa. You can use any extra as a dip with veggie sticks or crackers!

Yield: 3 cups

1	cup almonds, soaked in water for 8-12 hours, rinsed and drained		
1	cup sunflower seeds, soaked in water for 6-8 hours, rinsed and drained		
½	cup water	2	cloves garlic, minced
4	tablespoons lemon juice	2	tablespoons olive oil
2	tablespoons dulse flakes; if unavailable, use ½ sheet nori		
2	teaspoons salt	½	teaspoon black pepper
1	cup **Cashew Mayonnaise** (see page 58)	¼	cup finely chopped dill
½	cup each finely chopped celery and chive		

1. Place almonds and sunflower seeds in a food processor with water and process until well crumbled.
2. Add all the rest ingredients except for celery, chive and dill and process until well incorporated.
3. Transfer into the bowl, add celery, chive, and dill and mix evenly.

ITALIAN PASTAS AND EXOTIC VARIATIONS

East meets West!
Classic versus unique,
which one is your favourite?

How to Cook Pasta

Pasta is delicious on its own if you know how to cook. The key is the ratio of water to salt and "al dente" texture.

Yield: Serves 2

6	oz./160g pasta of your choice (3 oz./80g for 1 serving)
4	litres water
2	tablespoons salt (1% of the amount of water used)
1	teaspoon olive oil

1. Bring water to a boil with salt and olive oil.
2. Add pasta and stir gently until water boils again.
3. Reduce to low heat and simmer until "al dente," to be firm but not hard, then drain.

Pasta alla Marinara with Eggplant

Everybody's favourite classic!

Yield: serves 2

6	oz./160g pasta of your choice	4	tablespoons olive oil
1	clove garlic, sliced	½	fresh chilli, deseeded and sliced (optional)
1	Italian eggplant, diced	2	cups **Marinara Sauce** (see below)
10	olives, deseeded and sliced		

Garnish:

2-3 tablespoons **Cashew or Brazilian Nuts "Parmesan"** (see page 63)

2-3 tablespoons chopped parsley

1. Warm the olive oil in a pan with garlic and chilli on low heat until lightly brown and the aroma is released.
2. Add eggplant and sauté until golden brown.
3. Stir in olives and tomato sauce and cook for a few minutes.
4. Follow the directions on **How to Cook Pasta** (see page 99) to prepare pasta.
5. Put the pasta on a plate, then pour the sauce on top, and garnish with "parmesan" and parsley.

Marinara Sauce

There's nothing complicated about making delicious tomato sauce. The key is to cook slowly, gently, and patiently.

Yield: 3 cups

1	clove garlic, minced	1	onion, finely chopped
1	carrot, finely chopped	½	celery stalk, finely chopped
½	cup olive oil	1	teaspoon salt
2	teaspoons Italian dry mixed herbs		
28	oz./800g fresh or canned tomatoes, blended into puree		

1. In a saucepan, sauté garlic and onions in the olive oil over low heat for about 5 minutes or until slightly brown, then add carrot, celery, salt and herbs, and cook, covered, for 10-15 minutes.
2. Add tomato puree, bring to a boil over medium heat, and then reduce to the lowest heat and cook for about 30-45 minutes or until thickened.

Mushroom Cream Sauce Pasta

Cream + mushroom . . . it has been my long-time favourite! Mushrooms can be replaced by any veggies in season; my favourite is sweet pumpkin!

Yield: serves 2

6	oz./160g pasta of your choice	4	tablespoons olive oil
1	clove garlic, sliced or minced	½	fresh chilli, deseeded and sliced (optional)
4	cups assorted mushrooms of your choice, sliced or cut into bite-sized pieces		
2	cups **Non-Dairy Béchamel Cream Sauce** (see below)		

Garnish:

2-3 tablespoons **Cashew or Brazilian Nuts "Parmesan"** (see page 63)

2-3 tablespoons chopped parsley

1. Warm the olive oil in a pan with garlic and chilli on low heat until it becomes lightly brown and the aroma is released. Add assorted mushrooms and sauté until lightly brown.
2. Stir in non-dairy béchamel cream sauce and cook for a few minutes.
3. Follow the direction on **How to Cook Pasta** (see page 99) to prepare pasta. Fold the pasta into the sauce. Garnish with "parmesan" and parsley.

Non-Dairy Béchamel Cream Sauce

The perfect vegan béchamel sauce recipe! Once you taste it, there's no going back to buttery, heavy béchamel sauce. The key is to sauté the onion until brown slowly and then sauté the flour until completely cooked. Serve this over pastas, pizzas, tarts, and anything that you love!

Yield: 3 cups

½	cup olive oil	1	teaspoon mustard seeds
1	clove garlic, minced	1	onion, finely chopped
1½	teaspoons salt	2	teaspoons Italian dry mixed herbs
5	tablespoons wheat flour or spelt flour		24 oz. by volume/700ml soy/rice/nut milk

1. In a saucepan, heat the mustard seeds in olive oil over low heat.
2. When they start popping, add garlic and onion, sprinkle salt on top and cook, covered, over low heat for 3-5 minutes or until soft and slightly brown. Add herbs and cook for another few minutes.Add sifted flour and stir until well combined and cooked.
3. Slowly add soy/rice/nut milk, stirring little by little at a time over low heat.
4. Continue to cook, stirring, until the sauce thickens.

Marinated Hijiki and Tempeh Pasta

Hijiki + tempeh + olive + Asian dressing—its unique combination is my top recommendation!

Yield: Serves 2

6	oz./160g pasta of your choice
4	oz./110g tempeh, thinly sliced
1	handful hijiki, soaked in water for 30 minutes, drained
4	tablespoons olives, deseeded and chopped
1	cup broccoli florets, cut into small pieces and blanched
½	bell pepper, sliced

Marinade Sauce:

4	tablespoons olive oil
1	tablespoon soy sauce or tamari
1	tablespoon balsamic vinegar
1	clove garlic, minced
1	teaspoon Dijon mustard
1	teaspoon onion powder
1	tablespoon chopped fresh herb of your choice or 1 teaspoon dry herb
½	teaspoon salt

1. Panfry the tempeh with some additional oil on both sides until lightly brown, then crumble by hand.
2. For the marinade sauce, mix all ingredients in a bowl.
3. Marinate tempeh and hijiki in the marinade sauce for 30 minutes.
4. Follow the directions on **How to Cook Pasta** (see page 99).
5. Fold in the pasta, olive, broccoli, and bell pepper into the bowl of tempeh and hijiki mixture.

Japanese-Style Umeboshi Pasta

Intense sour-and-salty umeboshi is a pickled Japanese Ume plum. It is used in traditional Japanese cuisine but I found it works very well in pasta! Enjoy this delicacy of Japanese delight in a new style!

Yield: Serves 2

6	oz./160g pasta of your choice
10	Shiso leaves (Japanese basil), julienned; if unavailable, use Italian basil leaves
½	cup cherry tomatoes, cut into halves
4	tablespoons olives, deseeded and chopped
½	sheet nori, shredded

Umeboshi Cream Sauce:

4	large or 6 small umeboshi plums, deseeded
4	tablespoons deseeded and chopped dates
4	tablespoons tahini
4	tablespoons olive oil
½	cup water

Garnish:

2-3 tablespoons julienned Shiso leaves (Japanese basil); if unavailable, use Italian basil
Freshly cracked black pepper to taste

1. For umeboshi cream, mix all ingredients in a blender until smooth.
2. Follow the directions on **How to Cook Pasta** (see page 99) to prepare pasta.
3. Fold the pasta into the sauce with the rest of the ingredients.
4. Garnish with Shiso leaves and black pepper.

Raw Zucchini Pasta with Three Basic Raw Sauces

These are super easy to make! Each raw sauce can be used as a dip or spread for breads and crackers. Not only for raw zucchini pasta, these sauces are wonderful for usual pastas of course!

Yield: As much as you like

Zucchini, peeled

Any sauce of your choice from **Fresh Basil Pesto Sauce** or **Cashew Cheese Sauce** (see page 111) or **Quick Tomato Marinara Sauce** (see page 112)

Cashew or Brazilian Nuts "Parmesan" (see page 63)

1. Make zucchini into noodles with the spiral slicer (see FYI below).
2. Toss the zucchini pasta with sauce of your choice (top with other sauce if you like) and garnish with "parmesan" on top.

FYI: Serve immediately, as the water from zucchini will thin down the sauce. Alternatively, massage the zucchini noodles with salt, leave for 30 minutes, and then gently squeeze out the water and toss with the sauce so that the liquid won't come out.

FYI: The spiral slicer is great tool to turn any firm vegetable into fine, spaghetti-like strands or thin, long ribbons. It is a really fun gadget to play with and our staff at the retreats love it, so we have vegetable-noodle feasts every day.

If you don't have spiral slicer, slice zucchini lengthwise and then thinly slice lengthwise to make flat noodle shapes.

Fresh Basil Pesto Sauce

There are many recipes for pesto out there. Note that pesto is always made to taste, so adjust the ingredients and quantities to your taste. Try with different herbs and nuts to make it your original! Nutritional yeast creates cheesiness. It will last 1 month or more in the fridge.

Yield: 1¼ cups

3   cups packed basil

½   cup pine nuts or cashew nuts or nuts of your choice

½   cup olive oil

1-2 cloves garlic, crushed

1   tablespoon nutritional yeast

1   teaspoon salt or to taste

> **FYI:** The key is not to take too much time processing to adjust the flavour, as basil changes the color quickly. If it starts turning brown, add a bit more olive oil to keep it green.

1. Pulse all ingredients in the food processor until blended evenly but still chunky. Scrape down the ingredients rising up around the edges in between pulsing to get them evenly processed.
2. Transfer into a glass jar and cover the top completely with olive oil to prevent from the oxidation.

Cashew Cheese Sauce

This delicious cheese sauce without cheese has neither any milk or cream and even raw, and on top, the easiest to make! Even my friend who has been suspicious of raw food went crazy over this sauce. Not only for pasta, you can put it over fresh or steamed veggies, or serve with burgers or bread. Multi-purpose sauce!

Yield: 2 cups

2   cups cashew nuts, soaked in water for 2-4 hours, rinsed and drained

4   tablespoons olive oil

3   tablespoons lemon juice

2   tablespoons apple cider vinegar

2   tablespoons nutritional yeast; if unavailable, use white miso

½   teaspoon salt

½   cup water

1. Blend all ingredients in a blender until smooth.

Quick Tomato Marinara Sauce

Even if you're not going all out with the raw diet, this is a delicious, fresh, and easy sauce that you can have on the table in minutes.

Yield: 2 - 2½ cups

1   cup sun-dried tomatoes, soaked in water for 30 minutes, drained
1½   cups chopped tomato
½   cup olive oil
1   clove garlic, crushed
2   teaspoons Italian dry mixed herbs
½   teaspoon salt or to taste
      black pepper to taste

1. Process all ingredients in a food processor or blender until well incorporated

Asian Favourites

The most popular Asian ethnic dishes!

Chinese Sweet-and-Sour Stir-Fry

A Chinese-inspired tofu dish with sweet and sour sauce is always our guests' favourite. Great with rice or any other whole grains.

Yield: Serves 4

14	oz./400g firmed tofu (see **Firming Tofu** on page 22)
2	tablespoons sesame oil
2	tablespoons oil of your choice
2	cloves garlic, minced
1	tablespoon minced ginger
½	onion, cut into bite-sized pieces
1	bell pepper, cut into bite-sized pieces
1	cup each baby corns, broccoli, and pineapple, cut into bite-sized pieces
1	tablespoon Kudzu (arrowroot powder), dissolved in 4 tablespoons water

Sweet-and-Sour Sauce:

4	tablespoons rice vinegar or vinegar of your choice
4	tablespoons soy sauce or tamari
4	tablespoons coconut sugar syrup or sweetener of your choice
4	tablespoons **Raw Ketchup** (see page 59); if unavailable, use 3 tablespoons chopped & soaked sun-dried tomato)

1. For the sweet-and-sour sauce, mix all ingredients in a bowl. (If you are using sun-dried tomato, blend in a blender until smooth.)
2. Panfry tofu with the sesame oil on both sides until lightly brown and cut into 1 inch/2.5cm cubes.
3. Heat the oil of your choice in a wok.
4. Add garlic and ginger, stir for a few seconds until the aroma is released, then add the onions.
5. Stir briefly, add the bell pepper, baby corns, and broccoli, and stir for a few minutes.
6. Add sweet-and-sour sauce into the wok, turning up the heat.
7. When the sauce thickens a little, fold in the tofu and pineapple, and cook for a few minutes to heat through.
8. Stir the Kudzu mixture into the wok, stir for a minute or until the liquid becomes thick.

Balinese Tempeh Satay Skewers with Peanut Sauce

In Indonesia, grilled tempeh skewers are everywhere as street food snacks. Here, I've added an exotic sauce to make it into an impressive dinner! This simple peanut sauce is absolutely phenomenal, so you might want to make extra sauce to save to drizzle on other dishes.

Yield: 8 satay skewers

4.5 oz./125g tempeh, cut into 1.2inches/3cm squares

4 shiitake mushrooms, cut into halves

1 yellow bell pepper, cut into 1.2inches/3cm chunks

8 baby tomatoes

sesame oil and soy sauce or tamari to taste

Peanut Sauce:

½ cup roasted peanuts

2 cloves garlic, crushed

4 tablespoons coconut milk

2 tablespoons coconut sugar or sweetener of your choice

1 tablespoon soy sauce or tamari

1½ teaspoons lime or lemon juice

1 teaspoon onion powder

½ teaspoon chilli powder

½ teaspoon salt

1. For the peanut sauce, blend all ingredients in a blender until smooth.
2. Preheat the grill to medium heat.
3. Lightly toss tempeh and mushrooms with some sesame oil and soy sauce.
4. Thread mushroom, bell pepper, tempeh, and baby tomato onto each skewer.
5. Grill the skewers for 10-15 minutes on both sides until golden brown.
6. Serve with the peanut sauce.

FYI: If you don't have a grill, panfry all the items then thread onto skewers.

Baked Spring Roll with Sweet Peanut Dipping Sauce

This has been a big hit at my retreats! This sweet peanut dipping sauce is sensational.

Yield: 12-16 rolls

12-16 pieces of 8x8 inch/20x20cm Chinese spring roll wrappers (thawed if frozen)

Sesame oil to taste (to brush the wrappers)

Filling:

3	tablespoons sesame oil
2	cloves garlic, minced
6	shiitake mushrooms, thinly sliced
1	cup shredded cabbage
7	oz./200g firmed tofu (see **Firming Tofu** on page 22), crumbled by hand
¼	cup chopped green onions
2	tablespoons soy sauce or tamari
1	tablespoon coconut sugar or sweetener of your choice
½	teaspoon black pepper
½	teaspoon salt or to taste
1.7	oz./50g glass noodles
6	tablespoons ground white sesame seeds

Sweet Peanut Dipping Sauce:

4	tablespoons coconut sugar or sweetener of your choice
3	tablespoons rice vinegar or vinegar of your choice
½	teaspoon chilli flakes
½	cup water
4	tablespoons roasted peanuts, chopped

1. Soak glass noodles in boiled water for 3-5 minutes or until soft, wash in cold water, drain well, cut into 2 inch/5cm-sized pieces.

2. For the sweet peanut dipping sauce, cook all ingredients except for peanuts over low heat in a saucepan until half in volume, and then add peanuts.

3. For the filling, in a sauté pan, sauté garlic and mushrooms in the sesame oil over medium heat for a few minutes. Add all the rest of the ingredients except for the glass noodles and sesame seeds, and cook until all the liquid is evaporated.

4. Remove from the heat, mix in glass noodles and sesame seeds, and let it cool down.

5. Preheat oven to 400°F/200°C. Lightly grease a baking sheet or line with parchment paper.

6. To fold spring rolls, lightly brush both sides of each spring roll wrapper with sesame oil.

7. Place the wrapper like a diamond (the corner in front of you) on a clean, dry surface.

8. Place about 4-6 tablespoons of filling near the bottom corner, spreading it out sideways to form a rectangle shape but not touching the edges. (Try not to include too much of the liquid left in the filling.)

9. Lift the bottom corner of the wrapper and tuck it in under the filling. Fold over the left and right sides of the wrapper and roll over to the edge. Repeat with the remaining filling.

10. Place the rolls onto the baking sheet, facing the last edge of each roll to the bottom.

11. Bake in the oven for about 20 minutes or until slightly brown.

12. Serve with the sweet peanut dipping sauce.

Korean Savoury Pancakes

This is one of the most popular Korean dishes, "Chijimi," in a vegan version.

Yield: Serves 4

18 oz./500g daikon radish, julienned
1   teaspoon salt
2   cups fresh or frozen corn kernel (thawed if frozen)
2   cups garlic chives, cut into 2 inch/5cm pieces; if unavailable, use green onion
1   cup wheat flour or spelt flour
4   tablespoons Kudzu (arrowroot powder), dissolved in 3/4 cup water
½   teaspoon black pepper
    sesame oil as needed (for panfrying pancakes)

Korean Dipping Sauce:

3   tablespoons soy sauce or tamari
2   tablespoons sesame oil
2   tablespoons rice vinegar or vinegar of your choice
1   tablespoon coconut sugar syrup or sweetener of your choice
1   teaspoon each minced garlic, grated ginger, chopped chives, and chilli flakes

1. For the Korean dipping sauce, mix all ingredients in a bowl.
2. Place daikon radish in a bowl, massage with salt and leave it for a few minutes.
3. Add all the rest of the ingredients except for the sesame oil for panfrying and mix well by hand.
4. In a large flat pan, heat some sesame oil over a low flame.
5. Pour ¼ amount of mixture onto the pan.
6. Immediately spread and flatten them thinly and cook, covered, for 4-5 minutes.
7. Uncover and flip like a pancake.
8. Cook the other side for another 4-5 minutes without a cover.
9. Repeat with the remaining dough.
10. Cut into bite-sized pieces and serve with the Korean dipping sauce.

Pad Thai Noodle with Tofu-Egg

Here is a healthier and tastier version of the Thai classic, fragrant Thai stir-fry noodle! Another big hit at the retreats!

Yield: Serves 4

7	oz./200g flat rice noodles
4	tablespoons sesame oil
1	clove garlic, minced
1	tablespoon minced ginger
1	cup bean shoots (bean sprouts)
1	cup baby corns, cut into 1/4 lengthwise
1	red bell pepper, thinly sliced
1	cup green onion, cut into 2 inch/5cm lengths

Tofu-Egg:

7	oz./200g firmed tofu, crumbled by hands (see **Firming Tofu** on page 22)
2	tablespoons sesame oil
½	teaspoon black salt; if unavailable, use normal salt (see FYI below)
1	teaspoon soy sauce or tamari
½	teaspoon turmeric powder

Pad Thai Sauce:

6	tablespoons soy sauce or tamari
3	tablespoons coconut sugar syrup or sweetener of your choice
2	tablespoons lime or lemon juice
¼	teaspoon chilli flake
¼	teaspoon black pepper

Garnish:

6	tablespoons roasted peanuts, chopped
	Several lime or lemon wedges

1. Soak flat rice noodles in boiled water for 5 minute or until soft, wash in cold water and drain.
2. For the tofu-egg, heat the sesame oil over a medium flame, panfry tofu with the rest of the ingredients for a few minutes, transfer into a bowl and set aside.
3. For the Pad Thai sauce, mix all ingredients in another bowl.
4. In a large skillet, heat the sesame oil over medium heat.
5. Stir in garlic and ginger, then add all the vegetables and cook for a few minutes or until soft.
6. Add the Pad Thai sauce and bring to a simmer in a high heat.
7. Add noodles and cook, stirring frequently, until all the liquid is evaporated.
8. Fold in the tofu-egg, leaving some for garnish.
9. Garnish with peanuts and some tofu-egg and serve with lime wedges.

FYI: Black salt is high in sulfur, giving it an egg-y taste and smell.

"Yum Woon Sen" Thai Glass Noodles

I love its textures and flavours. All the fresh herbs, hot, spicy and sour dressing, and nutty, crunchy peanuts make it sensational.

Yield: Serves 4

4	oz./120g glass noodles
2	tablespoons sesame oil
5	shiitake mushrooms, thinly sliced
2	stalks celery, thinly sliced
1	each red and yellow bell pepper, thinly sliced
½	onion, thinly sliced
8	oz./220g **Teriyaki Tempeh** (see page 91)
1	cup cherry tomatoes, cut into halves
½	cup roasted peanuts, chopped
4	tablespoons chopped cilantro (coriander leaf)

Yum Woon Sen Sauce:

2	tablespoons sesame oil
3	cloves garlic, minced
8	tablespoons lime or lemon juice
4	tablespoons soy sauce or tamari
4	tablespoons coconut sugar syrup or sweetener of your choice
2	teaspoons salt
1	teaspoon chilli flakes

1. Soak glass noodles in boiled water for 3-5 minutes or until soft, wash in cold water, drain well, and cut into 4 inch/10cm pieces.
2. For the Yum Woon Sen sauce, mix all ingredients in a bowl.
3. Mix half of the sauce into the glass noodles and set aside.
4. In a pan, sauté shitake mushrooms, celery, bell pepper, and onion in the sesame oil over medium heat, drizzle the rest of the Yum Woon Sen sauce and cook for a few minutes.
5. Transfer into the glass noodle mixture and fold in all the rest of the ingredients.

Palak Paneer (Indian Curry with Spinach and Tofu-Cheese)

This is a vegan version of everybody's favourite Northern Indian feast! It is usually very heavy, but I kept it light and clean. "Palak" means spinach, and "paneer" is the Hindi word for Indian cottage cheese.

Yield: serves 6-8

6	cups packed spinach
4	tablespoons oil of your choice
2	teaspoons cumin seeds
2	cloves garlic, minced
1	tablespoon minced ginger
1	onion, finely chopped
1	tomato, finely chopped
2	teaspoons salt or to taste
1	teaspoon coriander seed powder
1	teaspoon cumin powder
1	teaspoon chilli powder or to taste
2	cups **Tofu-Ricotta Cheese** (see page 89)

Gravy Sauce:

2	onions, peeled
1	tomato
½	cup cashew nuts
2	bay leaves
1	cinnamon stick
1	teaspoon turmeric powder
2	cups water

Garnish:

2-3	tablespoons chopped cilantro (coriander leaf)
1	tablespoon finely julienned ginger

1. Lightly blanch the spinach, drain, and set aside.
2. For the gravy sauce, cook together in a pressure cooker; once the pins rise, turn the heat off, and leave it until the pressure is fully released. If you don't have a pressure cooker, cook all ingredients in a pot with ½ cup more water, covered, until the onion becomes completely soft.
3. Take out cinnamon stick and bay leaves, and blend with spinach in a blender until smooth.
4. In a soup pot, heat the cumin seeds in the oil over a low flame.
5. When the aroma is released, add garlic and ginger.
6. Add onion, sprinkle salt on top and cook, covered, over low heat for 3-5 minutes or until soft.
7. Add tomato and the rest of spices and cook for 10-15 minutes.
8. Add the spinach and gravy sauce mixture and cook until warm.
9. Fold in tofu-ricotta cheese, leaving some for garnish.
10. Garnish with cilantro, julienned ginger, and some tofu-ricotta cheese.

Sabuji (Curried Vegetables)

Sabuji is a cooked vegetable with Indian flavours. Sabuji sauce can be kept in the fridge for 2 weeks or more, so make a few batches and you can make different sabuji every day! Try with many other veggies. I like it with sweet veggies, such as pumpkin and sweet potato! Great accompaniment to chapatti and rice.

Yield: serves 4

6 cups any vegetable of your choice, boiled or steamed and large-diced
4 tablespoons coconut milk or as needed

Sabuji Sauce:

1   cup freshly grated mature coconut; if unavailable, use dry coconut
3   green chilies, deseeded and chopped, or to taste
1   tablespoon sliced ginger
1   tablespoon curry powder
³/₄ cup water
4   tablespoons oil of your choice
1   teaspoon mustard seeds
2   teaspoons cumin seeds
3   onion, thinly sliced
4   cloves garlic, minced
2   teaspoons salt
1   tablespoon coriander seed powder
1   teaspoon turmeric powder

1. For the sabuji sauce, process grated coconut, chilli, ginger, curry powder, and water in a food processor until pureed and set aside.
2. In a sauté pan, heat the mustard seeds in the oil over a low flame.
3. When they start popping, add cumin seeds, onion, garlic, and salt and cook, covered, over low heat until soft and slightly brown, then add pureed coconut mixture and the rest of the spices, cook over low heat for 5-10 minutes, stirring occasionally.
4. In a large pan, mix sabuji sauce and coconut milk.
5. Fold in the vegetables and cook for a few minutes. Add a little more coconut milk or water to achieve your favourite consistency if necessary.

Indian Eggplant Roll

This was a spontaneous accidental recipe and turned out to be a huge success!

Yield: Serves 4

3-4 Italian eggplants, sliced into 0.25 inch/0.7cm pieces lengthwise.

Oil of your choice as needed (for panfrying eggplant)

Filling:

1   cup **Rita's Coconut Chutney** (see page 59)

Garnish:

Freshly grated mature coconut or ground dry coconut as needed

1. In a large flat pan, heat the oil over a low flame.
2. Panfry eggplant slices until golden brown on each side.
3. Spread 1 tablespoon of coconut chutney lengthwise down the middle of each eggplant slice, leaving a 1 inch/2.5cm space at the end.
4. Beginning at the narrow end, roll up the eggplant.
5. Arrange the rolls onto serving plates, and sprinkle with ground coconut on top.

DESSERTS AND BREAKFAST BAKINGS

Egg-free, dairy-free vegan sweets for everyone! They are indeed quite surprisingly easy to make!

Buckwheat Pancakes with Banana and Tofu Whippy Cream

This is gluten free, white-sugar free, super healthy, and delicious! My favourite!

Yield: 6 of 4 inch/10cm diameter pancakes

1 cup buckwheat flour

1 teaspoon baking powder

pinch of salt

1 cup soy/rice/nut milk

1-2 tablespoons maple syrup or sweetener of your choice

1 teaspoon vanilla extract

coconut oil or oil of your choice as needed (for panfrying pancakes)

Serving:

Tofu Whippy Cream (see below) as needed

2-3 bananas, sliced into halves lengthwise, lightly sautéed in coconut oil

Maple syrup as needed

1. Sift the buckwheat flour, baking powder, and salt into a bowl and set aside.

2. In a separate bowl, mix soy/rice/nut milk, maple syrup, and vanilla extract, and then pour into the flour mixture and whisk until well incorporated.

3. Grease skillet with the oil over low heat.

4. Pour the 1/4 cup of batter and quickly spread into 4 inch/10cm-diameter circles.

5. Cover with a lid and cook for about 5 minutes or until many bubbles appear on top.

6. Flip and cook for another couple of minutes without cover. Repeat for the other pancakes.

7. Serve with sautéed banana and tofu whippy cream on top and drizzle with maple syrup.

Tofu Whippy Cream

As all my friends know, I love creaminess on literally everything! For cakes, muffins, and pancakes … simple, healthy, and the super-delicious cream takes you to the heaven. Guaranteed.

Yield: 1 1/2 cups

9   oz./250g firmed tofu (see **Firming Tofu** on page 22)

1.7 oz. by volume/50ml maple syrup

1.7 oz. by volume/50ml coconut milk

1   teaspoon vanilla extract

1. Blend all ingredients in a blender until smooth. Add a little additional coconut oil (melted if solid) or more coconut milk if necessary to facilitate easy blending.

FYI: If the cream consistency is still runny, add some additional coconut oil (melted if solid) to blend, which will help to set once it refrigerated.

Date Bars

Super delicious and nutritious! This is a great snack as well as a nice and healthy breakfast bar!

Yield: 12x8 inch/30x20cm squares

Oat Crust:

8   cups rolled oats

1   cup walnuts

½   teaspoon salt

½   cup coconut oil (melted if solid) or oil of your choice

½   cup maple syrup or liquid sweetener of your choice

Date Paste:

2   cups dates, deseeded and soaked in 3/4 cup water for 30 minutes

1   tablespoon lemon juice

1   tablespoon lemon zest

1. For the date paste, process all ingredients, including the date soaking water, into a paste in a food processer. Add a little more water if necessary to facilitate easy processing.
2. Preheat oven to 350 ° F/180 ° C. Lightly grease a baking pan or line with parchment paper.
3. For the oat crust, process the oats, walnuts, and salt in a food processor into powder.
4. Slowly add the coconut oil and maple syrup while pulsing.
5. Transfer into a bowl and mix by hand to combine the mixture evenly.
6. Spread half amount of the oat crust onto a baking pan and press down firmly.
7. Spread all the date paste on top of the oat crust evenly.
8. Place the rest of the oat crust evenly and press down firmly.
9. Bake 30 minutes or until golden brown on top.

Granola

Homemade granola is actually super simple to make and tastes amazing! Make variations with your favourite spices and flavours such as vegan chocolate chips, dried figs, or apricots. Enjoy with your favourite milk. It will keep for more than 1 month.

Yield: 9 cups

5	cups rolled oats
½	cup maple syrup
½	cup coconut oil (melted if solid) or oil of your choice
1	cup any seeds of your choice such as sesame seeds, sunflower seeds, pumpkin seeds
1	cup any nuts of your choice such as almonds, walnuts, hazel nuts
½	teaspoon salt
½	cup dry coconut
¼	cup raisins
¼	cup dates, deseeded and chopped
1	teaspoon cinnamon powder or vanilla extract

Serving:

Soy/rice/nut milk as needed

1. Preheat oven to 300 ° F/150 ° C. Lightly grease a baking sheet or line with parchment paper.
2. Mix rolled oats, maple syrup, coconut oil, seeds, nuts, and salt in a bowl until well combined.
3. Spread onto the baking sheet evenly.
4. Bake for 1 hour or more, stirring every 10-15 minutes to avoid burning at the edges.
5. Before turning brown, fold in all the rest of the ingredients and continue to bake until golden brown.
6. Serve with soy/rice/nut milk.

FYI: If you don't have an oven, panfry over the lowest heat, stirring occasionally.

Chocolate Banana Muffins

Chocolate and bananas . . . a never-go-wrong golden combination! Its freshly baked aroma is irresistible! The key is, once you mix the dry and wet ingredients, place into the oven straightaway! That ensures they'll rise up and makes fluffy, delicious cuties.

Yield: 6 muffins

Dry Ingredients:

- 7 oz./200g wheat flour or spelt flour
- 1 tablespoon baking powder
- ¼ teaspoon salt

Wet Ingredients:

- 4 oz. by volume/120ml maple syrup
- 2.7 oz. by volume/80ml coconut oil (melted if solid) or oil of your choice
- 1.7 oz. by volume/50ml soy/rice/nut milk
- ½ cup chopped vegan chocolate
- ½ banana, diced

1. Preheat oven to 350° F/180° C. Lightly grease muffin moulds.
2. Sift the dry ingredients into the bowl and set aside.
3. In a separate bowl, combine all the wet ingredients, then pour into the dry mixture, stir until just well enough combined.
4. Fold in chopped chocolate and banana.
5. Spoon into muffin moulds.
6. Bake 30 minutes or until golden brown on top.
7. Check with a toothpick by inserting it into the centre of the muffin. If it comes out clean, it is ready.

FYI: As it doesn't contain eggs, vegan muffins are best eaten the same day they're made. If they become dry the next day, you can make them into biscotti by slicing them and baking in the toaster!

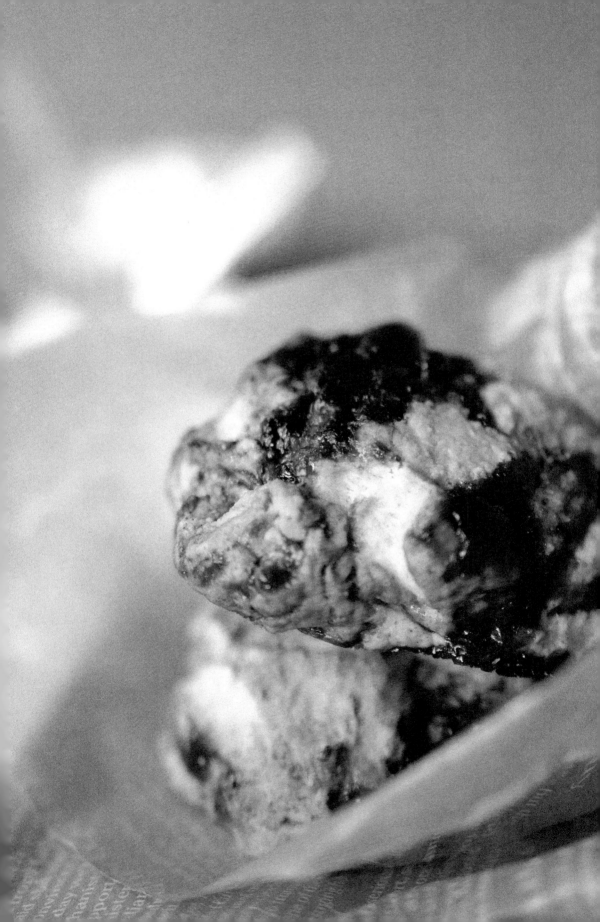

Peanut Butter and Blueberry Jam Scones

Another golden-winning combination, peanut butter + jam, brings me back to my childhood. Using the same technique as vegan muffins, the only difference is the quantity of the liquid, which determines scones or muffins. Now you know how easy it is to make delicious vegan cakes at home!

Yield: 6 scones

Dry Ingredients:

7   oz./200g wheat flour or spelt flour
1½ teaspoons baking powder
     pinch of salt

Wet Ingredients:

1.7 oz. by volume/50ml maple syrup
1.7 oz. by volume/50ml coconut oil (melted if solid) or oil of your choice
1.7 oz. by volume/50ml soy/rice/nut milk
3   tablespoons peanut butter
3   tablespoons blueberry jam

1. Preheat oven to 350 ° F/180 ° C. Lightly grease a baking sheet or line with parchment paper.
2. Sift the dry ingredients into the bowl and set aside.
3. In a separate bowl, combine all the wet ingredients, then pour into the flour mixture, stir until just well enough combined.
4. Fold in peanut butter and blueberry jam.
5. Using a large spoon, make 6 scone shapes onto a baking sheet.
6. Bake 20-30 minutes or until golden brown on top.
7. Check with a toothpick by inserting it into the centre of the scone. If it comes out clean, it is ready.

Chocolate Pie

I must admit, I was living on tofu desserts for quite some time in the past and I was literally like a piece of tofu! Watch out! This is thaaaaaaat good!

Yield: 9 inch/23cm pie

Easy Crust:

3   cups of your favourite vegan biscuits or cookies

3-4 tablespoons coconut oil (melted if solid) or oil of your choice

      pinch of salt

Chocolate Mousse Filling:

18 oz./500g firmed tofu (see **Firming Tofu** on page 22)

3.5 oz./100g coconut sugar or sweetener of your choice

7   oz. by volume/200ml coconut milk

4   tablespoons coconut oil (melted if solid)

1   teaspoon vanilla extract

7   oz./200g vegan dark chocolate, cut into small pieces

2   tablespoons cacao powder

Garnish:

Fruits of your choice as needed (optional)

1. For the easy crust, process biscuits in the food processor into powder.
2. Add the oil and salt until well incorporated. (Adjust the amount of the oil according to the softness of biscuits.)
3. Press into a lightly greased pie pan and keep it in the freezer until the filling is ready.
4. For the chocolate mousse filling, blend all ingredients in a blender except for the dark chocolate and cacao powder until smooth.
5. Add the dark chocolate and cacao powder and blend until dark chocolate is melted completely.
6. Pour into the crust, top with any fruits if desired, and refrigerate for a couple of hours or until set.

Perfect Tofu Cheesecake

You won't believe it has no dairy!

Yield: 9 inch/23cm cheesecake

Crunchy Crust:

2   cups granola of your choice (or use the granola recipe in this chapter)

$1/3$ cup walnuts

$1/8$ teaspoon salt

2   tablespoons coconut oil (melted if solid) or oil of your choice

1   tablespoon maple syrup

Cheesecake Filling:

14   oz./400g firmed tofu (see **Firming Tofu** on page 22)

3.5   oz./100g cashew nuts, soaked in water for 2-4 hours, rinsed and drained

6   oz. by volume/170ml maple syrup

½   cup lemon juice   1   tablespoon lemon zest

1   teaspoon vanilla extract   ½   teaspoon salt

1   teaspoon agar powder (or 1 tablespoon agar flakes)

5   oz. by volume/150ml coconut milk

Garnish:

Fruits of your choice or fruit puree as needed (optional)

1. For the crunchy crust, process granola, walnuts, and salt in a food processor into powder.
2. Add coconut oil and maple syrup and process until well incorporated.
3. Press into a lightly greased cheesecake pan, and keep it in the freezer until the filling is ready.
4. For the cheesecake filling, blend cashew nuts with maple syrup and lemon juice in a blender until smooth. Leave the mixture in the blender.
5. Heat agar powder and coconut milk in a small pot, bring to a boil while stirring, and simmer for 1 minute on low heat.
6. Pour into the cashew mixture in the blender, add all rest of the ingredients, and blend until smooth. (The agar mixture easily becomes solid. In case it sets before blending, heat again with about 2 tablespoons water to melt, then add quickly to blend.)
7. Pour into the crust, garnish with fruits or fruit puree if desired, then refrigerate for a couple of hours or until set.

Carrot Cake with Tofu Whippy Cream

So light and nutritious, it is perfect for breakfast!

Yield: 9x7 inch/23x18cm cake

12 oz./350g carrot, cut into big chunks

1 cup wheat flour or spelt flour

3.5 oz./100g almond powder

1½ tablespoons baking powder

¼ teaspoon salt

1 tablespoon cinnamon powder

1 teaspoon nutmeg powder

5 oz. by volume/150ml coconut oil (melted if solid) oil of your choice

1.7 oz. by volume/50ml maple syrup

2 oz./60g walnuts, chopped

3.5 oz./100g prunes, sliced and soaked in 2 teaspoons rum or vanilla extract

Garnish:

Tofu Whippy Cream as needed (see the recipe on page 131)

1. Preheat the oven to 350 ° F/180 ° C. Lightly grease a cake pan or line with parchment paper.
2. Process the carrot in the food processor into small pieces and set aside.
3. Sift the flour and baking powder into the bowl and mix with almond powder, salt, cinnamon, and nutmeg and set aside.
4. In a separate bowl, combine the oil and maple syrup, then pour into the flour mixture, add the carrot mixture, walnuts and prunes, saving a little of the walnuts and prunes to garnish, stir until just well enough combined.
5. Transfer into the baking pan.
6. Bake 30 minutes or until golden brown on top.
7. Check with a toothpick by inserting it into the centre of the cake. If it comes out clean, it is ready.
8. Spread the tofu whippy cream onto the carrot cake. Garnish with some walnuts and prunes.

Chocolate Fudge Ball

This is my number-one favourite bliss ball. Chocolate + walnuts, hmmm ... I'm in trouble, I can't stop it!

Yield: 20 of 1.4 inches/3.5cm bliss balls

2 1/2 cups walnuts

6 tablespoons cacao powder

4 tablespoons raisins

1 teaspoon vanilla extract

1/4 teaspoon salt

1 cup dates, deseeded and chopped

Garnish:

Cacao powder as needed

1. Process all the ingredients except for dates in the food processor.
2. Add dates gradually while processing until evenly combined.
3. Roll the mixture into small balls and coat with cacao powder.

Peanut Butter Balls

Who on earth does not like peanut butter? It makes anything taste good! Ha ha—but it's true! Everybody askes me what's in it! Now you know the secret ingredient!

Yield: 20 of 1.4inches/3.5cm bliss balls

2 cups granola of your choice (or use the granola recipe in this chapter)

1 cup dry coconut

1/2 cup non-sugar peanut butter

4 tablespoons orange marmalade

Garnish:

Dry coconut, powdered, as needed

1. Process granola and dry coconut in a food processor into powder.
2. Add peanut butter and orange marmalade and process until evenly combined.
3. Roll the mixture into small balls and coat with coconut powder.

Ingredients

Agar is a great vegan alternative to animal-derived gelatine. It is a gelatinous substance derived from red algae, widely used in Asia for soups and desserts. It is sold as bar or flakes or powder. One tablespoon of agar flakes is equal to 1 teaspoon of agar powder. To set 2 cups of liquid, use one bar, or 2 tablespoons of agar flakes, or 2 teaspoons of agar powder.

Amaranth is a tiny grain, originated in South America. It contains a high amount of protein and other minerals. Gluten-free.

Coconut sugar is made from the sap or nectar from the coconut palm tree flower. The best alternative to brown sugar (and white sugar of course), as it tastes similar to brown sugar with a bit of a rich caramel-like flavour.

Couscous is the smallest granule pasta, and originated in North Africa, where it is traditionally served with soups and stews.

Curry leaves are the leaves of the curry trees used in Southeast Asian cooking. They give a very distinct flavour and aroma to dishes. Although they are not related to curry powder at all, if it is difficult to find them, either omit or add some curry powder at the end to create an exotic flavour.

Dal is the Indian term for peas, beans, or lentils that have been split, but the name is sometimes used for the whole pea, bean, or lentil as well as cooked dishes made with it. It is often cooked into soups or puree.

Edamame is a young soybean in the pod, popular in Japan and China. It can be found in a health food shop or Asian grocery store. If unavailable fresh, it can often be found frozen.

Glass noodles, also known as cellophane noodles, mung bean noodles, or beans thread, are the type of Asian noodles made with mung beans, used in many Asian countries. They are used for fillings for dumplings and spring rolls, also used in stir-fries, soups, and salads.

Hijiki is a brown sea vegetable rich in minerals and fiber.

Kombu, edible kelp, is commonly used to make soup stock in Japan. It can be replaced by kelp powder.

Kudzu (arrowroot powder) is a Japanese arrowroot powder similar to tapioca flour and corn or potato starch. It is considered to improve body circulation and increase the yang energy in traditional Chinese medicine and macrobiotic systems.

Miso is a fermented soybean paste. The longer it is fermented, the more flavourful it is. It is important to choose unpasteurised miso, which has the beneficial bacteria alive.

Nutritional yeast is deactivated yeast cultured with sugar cane and/or beet molasses. It has a cheesy flavour and is often used as a cheese substitute in vegan dishes. If unavailable, most often it can be replaced with white miso.

Quinoa has been a staple in Andes for thousands of years. It is a seed, not a grain, but can be prepared like whole grains. It is a good source of minerals and fiber, as well as protein. Gluten-free.

Ragi, which looks like a black mustard seed, is an African millet also known as finger millet. Gluten-free.

Soba noodles are native Japanese noodles made of buckwheat flour (and sometimes mixed with wheat flour).

Spelt is an ancient species of wheat. It contains gluten, but in a small amount.

Spirulina, blue-green micro algae, has an amazing protein level of 60% on average, as well as many other nutrients.

Stevia is an herb that grows wild and is native to South America. It has 300 times the sweetness of sugar. It has no sugar and a glycaemic index of 0, so it does not raise blood sugar levels at all.

Superfoods are nutritionally dense foods, which offer tremendous dietary and healing potential.

Tempeh, fermented cooked soybeans, originated in Indonesia. The soy protein in tempeh becomes more digestible as a result of the fermentation process and contains beneficial bacteria.

Umeboshi is a pickled Japanese Ume plum with salt. Umeboshi are popular pickles and are sour and salty. They are usually served with rice or eaten on rice balls.

Wakame is a sea vegetable, which has a slightly sweet flavour and is most often served in soups and salads in Japan

Thanks to

... all my friends, I receive lots of love and power by sharing yummies with you!!

Lightning Source UK Ltd.
Milton Keynes UK
UKOW07f0312150817
307275UK00003B/27/P